1721 2021

300 Years

A Good Price for Fareham

A life in times of war, plague and fire

Paul Gover

1st edition 2022
2nd edition with amendments 2023

Published by The Society of Old Priceans
© Copyright 2022-2023 The William Price Charitable Trust

Preface to the second edition

After publishing this book in paperback, I returned to the Hampshire Record Office to make another attempt at reading and understanding the inventory taken after William Price senior's death. It is a particularly difficult example of "secretary hand", made much harder by inconsistent and error-strewn spelling.

The inventory (see Appendix B.2 on page 96) shows that the Prices had a comfortable cottage with a cooper's workshop and materials, in contradiction to my claim in the first paperback edition. This raises the question of why William Price junior did not take up his father's trade, and what happened to the cooperage business after his father's death. Sadly, I have no answers, only some speculations.

While at the Record Office, I found a contemporary picture of St Peter and St Paul's Church in Fareham, and was also able to track down the land which William junior left to Peter Price. It turns out to be a fairly small field in an area now adjacent to the A32 just north of the M27 motorway.

Kevin Price, a descendant of John son of John Price, contacted me with details of the marriage of William Price 1731?-1788 and Ann Jowles or Fowles, which proved the missing link in Deacon William Price's family tree (see page 52).

I have revised the text to include this new information, and added a short index consisting of important entries and surnames of people (other than Prices).

This edition of the book is set in digital versions of typefaces collected by Dr John Fell 1625-1686, Bishop of Oxford and Dean of Christ Church for use by the Oxford University Press. William Price may well have read books printed using them.

Paul Gover
March 2023

Preface

William Price was probably Fareham's greatest benefactor. He left most of his estate to found a "Bluecoat" charity school for the town's poor children. There are no portraits or statues of William Price; he left no diary. The only sample of his handwriting is his signature to his will; even there, the rest was written by legal professionals.

Little has previously been written about him. At the time of writing, he appears in neither the Encyclopaedia Britannica nor Wikipedia. This book is an attempt to give a glimpse of both his and his father's life and times. It is published as part of the Society of Old Pricean's celebration of the 300th anniversary of the foundation of Price's school.

The story covers turbulent times - the Civil War, the Commonwealth, the Great Plague, the Restoration of the Monarchy, and Britannia's efforts to continue to rule the waves - events with great impact on their home towns of Titchfield and Fareham.

About the cover photograph

The cover photograph is of trees in the grounds of Fareham Leisure Centre. The grounds lay directly across Park Lane from the site where Price's School moved in 1908. The land on which the Leisure Centre is built was once known as Butterwick. William Price owned Butterwick, and it is mentioned in his will. William will have walked here, perhaps kept a horse on the adjacent purrock, and possibly even sold timber from trees growing on it 300 years ago.

Acknowledgements

Thanks for their help and patience to the staff at The National Archives, the Hampshire Record Office and Portsmouth History Centre. Thanks for permission to use images of their items to the Hampshire Record Office, the Hampshire Cultural Trust and The National Archives Image Library. Thanks to the members of the Society of Old Priceans for encouragement, information and suggestions. Thanks to the Titchfield History Society for having published transcriptions of Titchfield parish records. The Fell Types are digitally reproduced by Igino Marini www.iginomarini.com

And thanks to my wife Sheila for her insights and support during this book's development.

Contents

Illustrations

Family trees

1 Introduction

This story of William Price's family is pieced together from few sources containing only a few hard facts. St Peter and St Paul's Church Fareham contains the Prices' memorial. The Hampshire Record Office in Winchester contains his and his father's wills and part of the manorial court roll recording the ownership of a cooper's shop. The National Archives has chancery rolls concerning challenges to the will. *The History of the English Baptists,* Joseph Ivimey (1830) relates a tale about the founder of Price's School. The Titchfield History Society published St Peter's Church parish register of baptisms, marriages and burials. The Internet, especially findmypast.com and ancestry.com, provides more parish records and a few relevant apprenticeship documents.

Anyone researching a family history since the advent of the Internet will know the wealth of information available from the 19th Century, particularly the census returns, the backbone to any skeleton family tree. But the pickings are meagre in the 17th and early 18th centuries.

We used to have detailed information from tombstones and memorials, but over the last few decades many of these have been moved or suffered from acid rain erosion. The Hampshire Genealogy Society's records of monumental inscriptions for Fareham and Titchfield contain only the already mentioned memorial relevant to this story. Apprenticeship records are valuable but incomplete. The level of detail in parish registers varies according to the conscientiousness of the parish clerk, and further, the story crosses the period known as the "commonwealth gap" in genealogical records.

The story below would never stand up in a court of law; it is conjecture from the memorial and wills, circumstantial evidence from the court roll and registers, and hearsay from Ivimey, along with an icing of reading between the lines. There is almost no corroboration between the components. But the story is consistent with all the sources, and may explain why William Price of Fareham did not follow his father's trade of cooperage, and bequeathed the considerable estate he amassed to found Price's School rather than enrich all his nearest relatives.

Where applicable, this book converts dates in the old church calendar with the year ending on 25th Match to the modern calendar.

The family trees in this book are compressed to fit on the page. Where a name appears with one date below it, it's their birth year; a marriage is indicated by the names separated by either a couple of equals signs containing the year, or just one equals signs if it's not known; question marks attached to a year means a guess, standing alone means unknown.

The two main protagonists, William Price, father and son, are distinguished throughout this book by the suffices "senior" and "junior", usually abbreviated as "sen." and "jun."; similarly one "John Price, son of John Price" is usually "John jun.". It is unlikely they used these suffices during their lifetimes - they typically appear only when they might be needed to distinguish them from other Prices, such as in parish records. Of course, over time in a family where the first-born son is given his father's name, juniors may become senior. However, throughout this book William Price junior will always identify the founder of Price's School, and William senior his father.

The maps show extracts from the 1840 Hampshire Tithe Apportionment maps from the Hampshire Record Office, combined with present day (2022) maps (© OpenStreetMap contributors) from the Open Street Mapping project. Land owned by the Prices or the Charity is shown in black, as are the two big plots in Elson sold to the Board of Ordnance, later the site of Priddy's Hard and the Magazine.

1.1   Historical Record Sources

This book makes frequent reference to two sources of records in particular: The National Archives, abbreviated as TNA, and the Hampshire

Record Office, abbreviated as HRO. References to their documents are shown in brackets "[…]".

Along with the parish records of births, marriages and deaths, this book makes use of wills, the manorial fine books and the 1840 tithe apportionment.

Wills

A will can be quite informal - a sheet of paper drawn up at the testator's sickbed, or formal - a similar but more expensive document drawn up by a lawyer. The only requirement is that it is properly witnessed. Wills can be very useful in historical research, as they describe peoples' relationships, often confirming details that can only be surmised from the normally very terse parish records.

Fine books

The fine books recorded the tax due on various transactions on within the manor, most notably when property changed hands. In the 16th and 17th centuries, much of the law of land was *copyhold* - owned by the lord of the manor, and leased to tenants. The manor recorded a copy of the tenant's title to the land on the manorial rolls. The manor levied a *fine* or tax every time the tenancy changed, including on sale, marriage or death. There is no suggest of illegality in this use of "fine".

The HRO holds a large collection of the fine books for various manors, and very usefully indexes to the fine books for several manors compiled by patient researchers, perhaps in Victorian times. These indexes provide a concise extract of the parties and fines levied all in one book in English - the fine books themselves being in very abbreviated Latin before 1733. The fine book index for Fareham borough [HRO 11M59/C4/2/11/1] is particularly useful.

The 1840 Tithe Apportionment Maps

Alongside the manorial fines due when the title-holder changed, tenants had to pay the rector tithes, originally one tenth of the produce from the land. This custom was finally abolished by the 1836 Tithe Commutation Act, which replaced the tithe with a monetary payment. This required commissioners to map the manors and draw up lists of who paid what and to whom for which land. The HRO holds these maps and lists [HRO 21M65/F7], and also publishes them on CD-Rom.

Chancery Bills and Answers

The National Archives holds records from the Court of Chancery, which heard cases concerning "equity", or rather inequity, An *Orator* would plead their case that they had been treated unfairly in a *Bill* before the court. The defendants would reply with an *Answer*, which could then be challenged with a further pleading. These were civil cases, not legal ones - the law had not been broken, but there was inequity. Typical cases covered the provision or interpretation of wills, and breaches of contract.

The records are mostly court rolls - huge sheets of vellum covered in notes written by scriveners. They had to be very repetitious, as the photocopier would not be invented for centuries, so for example every discussion of a will would need large parts of the said will copied into the court records, with the witnesses to the will swearing the veracity of the copies.

2 William Price senior, cooper of Titchfield

Here lyeth the Body of William Price, Senior who departed this life June 12th 1665 in the 48th year of his age. — part of the inscription on the Price family's memorial in St Peter and St Paul's parish church in Fareham.

Our story of William Price, founder of Price's School, starts with his father, also William. The only recorded baptism of a William Price in Hampshire in 1617 was on 29th June in St Peter's Titchfield.

The Titchfield parish register sporadically records a baby's father's name throughout the 16th and early part of the 17th centuries, but they do not give William Price sen.'s parents' names. William Price jun.'s will shows he had many cousins and kin, and as he had only two siblings and no children, it seems his father came from a large family of Prices in Titchfield. The likely family is that of John Prise and Margaret Waller of Titchfield.

Spelling was pretty informal in those days. The name "Price" is usually from Wales, "Ap Rhys", son of Rhys, and gets spelled variously as Price, Prise, Pryce, Prysse and similar. It is a common name in England, but as Rhys was a popular Welsh name, different Price families are unlikely to be related. The register shows another two baptisms, for Marcye in 1606 and John in 1608 with father Nicholas Price, but there is no marriage record and this family never appears again. The marriage registers for the rest of Hampshire show no other suitable candidates.

The first record of John and Margaret is their marriage in St Peter's church on 27th September 1601. The register lists Price baptisms for John jun. 1602, Nicholas 1605 (who died in infancy), Christopher 1609, Marcy 1611, William in 1617, Sarah 1619, Frances 1622 (who also died in infancy) and lastly Ellen in 1624.

We also need a Peter Prise, but his baptism is not recorded. It seems likely he was part of the same family; we know "Peeter Prise" married Ann Knight in 11th July 1642 in Titchfield, "Peter son of Peter Price" was William Price's kinsman, and a Peter Price is described as coopar [*sic*] on his burial in Titchfield 1665. He would fit neatly into the family with a birth about 1614. A family tree based on this information can be seen on the next page.

The Prises or Prices may have been the town's coopers (barrel makers); William sen. was a cooper in Fareham by the time he made his will. We know little of the rest of the family; Christopher seems to have moved to Bishop's Waltham, John Prise was buried at the start of 1662 and his widow Margaret 9 months later.

2.1   May you live in interesting times

The claimed Chinese curse could well apply to William Price sen. - he was born into one of the most turbulent times in English history, in no small part down to religion.

Titchfield Abbey, Place House and the Earls of Southampton

Titchfield has a long history - the Doomsday book mentions a mill there worth 20 shillings. Titchfield is believed to have been an important and wealthy mediaeval port for the nearby 13th century monastery. Documentary evidence such as reports of cargo dues or customs revenue are missing and timber from Titchfield Park is recorded being carried to Fareham quay, not shipped from Titchfield; perhaps the port's trade was fairly local. Henry VIII dissolved the monastery in 1537 and granted its estate along with Beaulieu Abbey's to Lord Thomas Wriothesley. He used its stone to build a stately home "Place House" on the site now called Titchfield Park (English Heritage's "Titchfield Abbey" ruins).

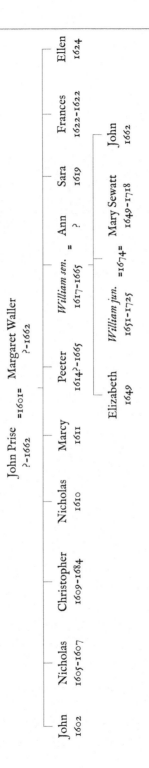

William Price (father and son)

Place House, Titchfield, 1733
from an engraving by S. & N. Buck

The earl appears to have been an ambitious, ruthless and thoroughly unpleasant man. He personally operated the rack on Anne Askew, a Protestant, one of two women to have been tortured in the Tower of London. On the King's death, Wriothesley was created 1st Earl Southampton. As a Catholic, he may have been unpopular with his Protestant neighbours in Titchfield; one version of the origin of the Titchfield Bonfire Boys is that it is his effigy they burn each year.

His son Henry Wriothesley entertained Edward VI and later Elizabeth I and their courts at Place House. The 2nd earl was also a Catholic; his part in the Northern Rebellion against the Queen was not punished, but his activities lead him to spend 18 months as a prisoner in the Tower.

The 3rd Earl, another Henry, was a far better man than his grandfather. He achieved fame as the dedicatee of two of Shakespeare's sonnets, and it is probable he supported him financially, and several other authors dedicated works to him. He too was an intriguer, and was sentenced to death for his part in Essex's rebellion (with aims including ensuring James VI of Scotland succeeded to the English throne) in 1601. The sentence was commuted to life imprisonment, and after the Queen died, James (now also James I of England) returned him to court.

Outside the park, Titchfield had gained from the Wriothesley family's wealth to become an important market town. But by the time of John and Margaret Prise, it was no longer so wealthy and the harbour had silted up. Europe was entering the coldest part of the "Little Ice Age", with farming becoming ever harder.

The 3rd Earl, an enlightened landlord, sponsored industries around Titchfield, including wool weaving and the iron works at Funtley in 1621, where a century later Henry Cort would in-

Henry Wriothesley 3rd Earl Southampton, after Daniel Mytens

vent his puddling process for the production of iron. He may have created England's second-oldest canal that runs from the town to the sea at Titchfield Haven as early as 1614. However, more recent research published in the Titchfield History Society's *Titchfield an Ancient Parish* (2011) provides evidence supporting a later date around 1675, and that the 1614 work was more likely to do with a sea wall by the Haven. The canal may have been used to carry produce after the Meon's estuary silted up, though again there is no documentary evidence; perhaps it was an irrigation system or even a large millstream. He was involved in the East India Company and the New World Company, and bright, entering St John's college Cambridge at the age of 12; all in all, a bit of a polymath.

2.2 William Price senior's early life under King Charles I

John and Margaret Prise's family life at the start of the 17th century was in a period of great change. There are no records specific to the Prices; instead we must look to the events of the times. The Catholics failed to destroy parliament in the famous Gunpowder Plot of 1605. King James I's accession to the throne united England and Scotland. His Authorised Version Bible was published in 1611, helping to cement Protestantism in England. Abroad, Copernicus and Galileo's works on the nature of the universe so challenged the orthodox view that the Catholic Church banned them in 1616, a year before William sen.'s birth. He was three when the Mayflower called in at Southampton on its way to Virginia in the New World.

In 1625, when William sen. was eight, James I died and Charles I succeeded to the throne. Soon after, the parish register says in August *"King Charles and Queene Mary came to Titchfield place the xxth day this moneth and the Queene stayed there five weekes & Three dayes"*, while avoiding an outbreak of plague in London. It is unlikely there would be a royal procession as we would have these days; the new Queen, who preferred her full name Henrietta Maria, was deeply unpopular as she was a French Catholic. Her Catholic court would not have endeared itself to the Titchfield locals after one member fired a shot at the Protestant vicar, who had already received death threats.

The King was soon funding wars with France and Spain, and imposed unpopular measures such as martial law and billeting the military in private homes. His equally unpopular right-hand man George Villers, Duke of Buckingham, lead the Navy to defeat at La Rochelle. The Titchfield parish register of 1628 records *"The Lorde Duke of Buckingehame was slayne at Portesmouth the 23rd day of Auguste beinge lattersday Generall of all the fleete by sea and land whose name was George Villers Right Honerable"*. He was assassinated in the Greyhound pub, now ironically called Buckingham house, by disgruntled army officer John Fenton. Fenton became a popular hero despite, or maybe because, after his hanging at Tyburn his body was taken to Portsmouth for public display.

Charles and Henrietta stayed again in Place House after the birth of the future Charles II in 1630. In 1635, Henry Wriothesley was selling the Navy timber from Titchfield Park. In 1636, Charles levied "ship money" (a fee he could demand without Parliament's authority) across the country, including £50 from Fareham, and in 1638 the King demanded that Fareham supplied a ship of 400 tons and 160 crew to be ready in Portsmouth within 4 months.

Apprentice cooper

For much of this time, William Price sen. would have been an apprentice indentured to a master cooper. The conditions of apprenticeship were virtual slavery, albeit for only seven years - ordered about by their master, unable to leave, marry, or drink alcohol and almost unpaid, all enforced by the law. Unlike being sold into true slavery, an apprentice had to buy into it! That had the merit for us of sometimes leaving records giving the apprentice's name and parent and the master's name and craft - the indentures. After 1709, indentures were taxed, and hence kept by the taxman, but that is too late for William's indenture, and none remains.

Apprenticeships were compulsory for anyone who hoped to enter a trade. The Poor Law allowed the parish overseers to apprentice a child under 14 whose parents could not maintain it. In William's case it is possible his father took him in apprenticeship, a common practice, and presumably he would have been rather better treated. William's will says he was a cooper, and his presumed brother Peter's burial in 1665 records him as a coopar [sic], so cooperage appears to have been the family trade. Apprenticeship typically lasted at least seven years, until boys were 24, girls 21. Girls were rarely apprentices in the trades, but a much higher percentage of "pauper" or "parish" apprentices were girls, though only learning "housewifery".

Apprentices lived as part of their master's household. They learned by example and practice; an efficient and cost-effective process, but not one that encouraged change or improvement in the techniques employed. There could be a religious aspect too; God's creations were perfect, and it was not for man to attempt perfection or to try to improve on God's work. Techniques such as clock-making remained unchanged despite improved scientific understanding. Coopers made barrels the same way for centuries; even today there is an artisan cooperage trade that William would recognize in its entirety, the only change being industrially-produced tools.

When his apprenticeship completed in about 1642 William would be free to move to Fareham and call himself a journeyman cooper, and later rise to become a master cooper. Titchfield at the time would have been a busy town, but still very quiet compared to modern days. William would have been able to hold a conversation with customers or passers-by while he worked in the cooperage, with only the sound of hand tools, or the occasional thump of a mallet instead of the modern whirl of electric motors. The air would be full of the noise of children playing and the clatter of horseshoes and iron-shod wheels on cobbles instead of the throb of car and van engines. Perhaps William might escape the hustle and bustle of the town for the peace of the fields a few hundred yards away, where the only sounds would be the soaring skylark's song punctuated by the distant blacksmith's hammer. But on Wednesday, 20th August, he would hear a louder thunder from far off.

2.3 The Civil War in Hampshire, and Lord Goring

One of the war's earliest actions was the Siege of Portsmouth, which must have affected the people of Fareham and Titchfield. It started in August 1642 with troops massing and small skirmishes. The Parliamentarian forces started a naval blockade and prepared a gun platform in Gosport, and on the 20th the canons opened fire on the Portsmouth garrison.

Lord George Goring, the eldest son of the 1st Earl of Norwich (also a Lord Goring), commander of the Portsmouth garrison, deserves mention. Having fought as a Colonel in the Dutch army, Goring had a reputation as an able fighter, and a prodigious drinker! He served in Charles I's army in the "Bishop's Wars" against the Scottish Presbyterians in 1639 and 1640, enhancing his reputation. At this point, he was involved in the "Army Plot" of 1641, in which he proposed a Royalist force from York would march on parliament and the Tower of London. However, his fellow officers refused to support him, so Goring then betrayed the plot to Parliamentarian supporters! Styling himself Colonel Goring (the Parliamentarians recognised no courtesy titles) he gave evidence to the Commons, who commended him on his services to the Commonwealth - i.e., the Parliamentarian side. They sent him back to command the Portsmouth Garrison (the mayor and people there were Parliamentarian supporters), with money to improve its defences. To which, it was rumoured, he added money from the Crown!

By August 1642 he had come out on the Royalist side - just in time for the Siege of Portsmouth. Parliamentarian forces blockaded the island from the north, and seven warships prevented relief from the Solent. Royalists in Fareham sent food. The garrison had one warship, the *Henrietta Maria*, but the Parliamentarians captured it and took it to Fareham. By the beginning of September, the Parliamentarians were bombarding Portsmouth from Gosport, Southsea Castle, and Portsea. Lord Goring (as the true Royalist now styled himself) negotiated a surrender by threatening to blow up the magazine and the town with it. He promised to hand over the magazine intact in return for safe passage for himself and his remaining troops. As he left for the Netherlands, he threw the keys to the town into the Solent.

While abroad he raised troops for the Royalists, returning to England by December, fighting at the battles of Seacroft Moor and Marston Moor. At the start of 1645, he was back in Hampshire with 3,000 troops, establishing an outpost in Fareham by the 9th January. However, he could not hold it and fell back to Salisbury. *The Civil War in Hampshire* by Rev. G.N. Godwin (1904) says *"After burning about twenty-five houses at Gosport, he marched westward, driving off all the cattle, horses, sheep, swine, and carrying away many men out of the hundreds of Titchfield, Alverstoke, and Fareham."* William sen., a tradesman with a tough, physical job as a cooper aged just 28 would have been a prime target for Goring's press gangs, if he was not already in some fighting unit. In March, the Parliamentarian force of Norton's Horse stayed briefly in Titchfield during their pursuit of Goring's forces. There are no records of William fighting on either side, but then there are few such records of any commoners; history was written by the nobility and the officers. If William had moved to Fareham, it is even possible he was dragged into the fighting on the opposite side to his relatives from Titchfield - brother against brother.

This first civil war ended with the Royalist army's final defeat in 1646. The following year, King Charles escaped from Hampton Court and visited Place House yet again on his way to Carisbrooke, where he hoped the Isle of Wight's governor would shelter him. However, the governor imprisoned him there. The brief second civil war in 1648 also ended with defeat of the Royalists. In 1649 parliament beheaded Charles I, and England entered the Interregnum.

3 The Price family in Fareham

With the expansion of seaborne trade in the 16ᵗʰ century and the growth of the Navy under Henry VIII, casks were in great demand. The coopering craft enjoyed great prosperity, supplying casks for everything that had to be stored on board ship - food, drink, ammunition and cargo, and it is only in fairly modern times that 'cooper' ceased to be a rating in the Navy – the Worshipful Company of Coopers.

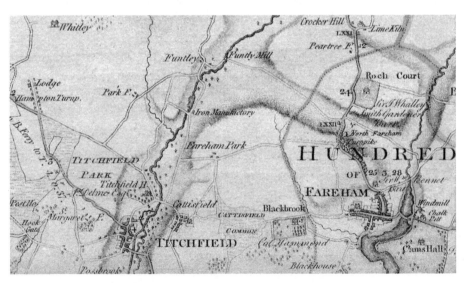

Titchfield and Fareham from Milne's 1791 map
Hampshire County Museums Service.

William had a valuable trade in a port; by now 32, he was married and living in Fareham with a baby daughter Elizabeth, baptised on 20th April 1649. Sadly, this is all we know about her apart from mention in her father's will.

Fareham was still pre-industrial; Henry Cort would not revolution-ize iron smelting in Funtley for another hundred years, and the potteries and brickworks would only flourish after the railway arrived around 1840. The tidal mill at Cams was already old; Wallington was known for its tanneries; the inhabitants of Hampshire (or the County of Southampton, as it was called) were largely employed in agriculture - Fareham had a weekly market. The equivalent of modern motorway and rail transport was coastal shipping, and Fareham was a significant harbour for the Royal Navy, and commercial port for timber from Titchfield Park sent to Gosport and Portsmouth dockyard.

Fareham's population was only about 750, and the town consisted of a short section of what is now East and West Street, intersected by High Street and Quay Street. North Road went up what is now Old Turn-pike, and West Street went through Catisfield, over the narrow Stoney Bridge to Titchfield - the new turnpikes to Wickham and Titchfield, now the A32 and A27, were not built until around the turn of the 19th century. The parish church was St Peter and St Paul's, as it had been for centuries, though it looked very different without the 19th and 20th century additions, and Holy Trinity Church would not be built in West Street until the 19th century.

Charles II's forces' defeat at the Battle of Worcester on 3rd Sept. 1651 marked the last action of the Civil War. On the 10th October 1651 William Price jun.'s baptism is recorded in St Peter and St Paul's parish register; thus he was born into the first Commonwealth. By the time he was four, Oliver Cromwell had dissolved parliament and installed himself as Lord Protector for life, in the manner of so many revolutionaries. While the Hampshire nobility's power and influence would be affected by the Parliamentarian victory directly during the coming decade, for a family of commoners like the Prices the likely impact was more from puritanism. Like religious fundamentalists today, the puritans disap-proved of music, entertainment and immodest dress and enforced strict religious observance, suppressing theatres and proscribing holidays such as Christmas and Easter. That said, puritanism made little progress in

St Peter and St Paul's Fareham, about 1707; [HRO 65M89/Z90/7]

previously Royalist areas such as Fareham; perhaps not much changed when Charles II was restored to the monarchy in 1660.

On 19th April 1662, William's last child John was baptised. Unfortunately, John is a common Christian name, and there are several John Prices in south Hampshire at this time, so nothing is known for certain about him.

3.1 Mrs Price

> *All the rest of my goodes & chattelles I give and bequeath unto my Loving wife Ann Price whome I make constitute & ordayne to be my full & Sole Executrix* – William Price sen.'s will.

There is a surprisingly large gap between William's and John's baptisms. No Price children appear in the parish register in the 11 years between them, not even children dying in infancy. We do not know the children's mother - the baptisms list only the father's name "Willm" - nor are any marriages listed for William Price in the parishes in the Fareham and Titchfield area that fit the timescale. Unfortunately, this period lies in the "Commonwealth Gap", when Cromwell's parliament tried to replace church records with civil ones, so records are unreliable.

It is possible Elizabeth and William jun.'s mother died and William sen. remarried, making John their stepbrother; we only know that at the time of William sen.'s will in 1665, his wife was Ann.

> *I Comend my Soule to God and my Body to the Earth to be buried in a Decent manner under the Stone my Father and mother Lye in Fareham Church yard* – William jun.'s will.

Despite the words in William Price jun.'s will, the inscription on his memorial in St Peter and St Paul's churchyard does not mention his mother. The stone now on the memorial has been renovated at least once, but it looks in surprisingly good condition for its 300 years age. It may have been replaced by the Edwardians when Price's School moved to Park Lane in 1908; it shows the same Lion coat of arms as the school badge, and that may be a Victorian invention. It is common for such "chest tomb" memorials to be built after the original burial and in a different place. The tomb may be empty, and the stone under which the Price family's bodies lie may be elsewhere in the churchyard, so damaged by erosion to be illegible.

3.2   The family home

William sen.'s will gives a sense of the Price family's life: it mentions "the chamber over the hall", so they lived moderately well, in a house with a room grand enough to call a hall, and it mentions some land. The 1665 hearth tax records have William Price living in Cams Oysell (the old name for the south-east side of Fareham) with two taxable hearths. This makes the Prices neither rich nor paupers; the poor either did not have hearths or were excused paying the hearth tax; the comfortably off are reckoned to have at least three hearths.

The estate inventory transcribed in Appendix B.2 on page 96, made after William's death, shows the house to be a typical artisan's cottage, with a kitchen and hall on the ground floor and a room above. Its furnishings are comparatively luxurious with feather-filled mattresses and pillows; there's a well-equipped kitchen too. Then there is a shop and a workhouse, presumably some sort of outhouse on the same land, containing William's cooperage products, tools and materials. The Prices also have a three-acre field growing barley at the time. This appears to be one of two fields that William bought in 1662, filling much of the triangle between Blind Lane (now Hartlands Road) and West Street now lying under the Fareham bus interchange (see the map on page 68).

3.3 The Great Plague of London (and Hampshire)

> *We whose names are hereunto subscribed being present with William Price of Fareham in the County of Southampton on the eleaventh day of June Anno Domini 1665. The said William Price being sicke in body but of Sound and perfect memory Did declare & make his last will and testament*

[This section uses Julian dates, as those were in use at the time; Samuel Pepys's diary calls 11th June 1665 a Sunday, whereas a modern website will use the Gregorian calendar and say it is a Tuesday.]

William sen. dictated his will "sicke in body" on Sunday 11th June 1665; the memorial says he died Monday 12th June and the parish register says he was buried Tuesday 13th June 1665 in Fareham. There is a story here in itself.

1665 marked the last major outbreak of bubonic plague in Great Britain. It spread across Europe starting around 1660, reaching the Netherlands ports by 1663. As the plague approached, England introduced 40 days quarantine (hence the word) for Dutch shipping. By April 1665, the first house in London was sealed up; by July, the plague was rampant in London, and those who could obtain a certificate of good health fled to the country. (The similarities to the 21st century's COVID-19 outbreak are striking.) Drivers took their carts through the city, crying "Bring out your dead"; the bodies were thrown into plague pits. At its peak there were over 7,000 recorded deaths a week; many more went unrecorded. In total, between 70,000 and 150,000 died in London.

It's remembered as the Great Plague of London, but it spread outside. Reputedly, a child from London brought it to Southampton in June 1665, killing 30-40% of the inhabitants by the end of the year. *The Great Plague* by Stephen Porter (2009) says:

> *Plague may have made an early appearance in the Hampshire towns at Fareham, where the number of burials began to rise in May 1665, continuing at an abnormally high level during June and into early July. The disease continued to claim victims there until September 1666, but the pattern was erratic. ... The total number of burials in 1665 was 56, and the following year 79, the highest for any year since the plague of 1563.*

The normal level of deaths in Fareham was more like 15 a year at that time. The speed of William sen.'s demise and burial suggests he died of the plague.

(A popular defence against plague then was smoking the new-fangled tobacco from America. Tomatoes, now part of the healthy "Mediterranean diet", were considered poisonous. How times change.)

The will named William's wife Ann, and three children Elizabeth, William and John. In *The History of Price's School* 1721-1971 F.E.C. Gregory says of William sen. *"he must have been quite a prosperous craftsman as his estate was worth £32 10s. 0d."* and *"William received the largest bequest of all the children as he was the eldest son.".* Both deductions are erroneous. William Price's father was not a rich man: in 2021's money, he left bequests of about £4,500, and an estate valued about £5,000. The family house was reasonably comfortable with two hearths, but still only a cottage.

William's sister Elizabeth, sixteen at the time of her father's death, was left the best bed and bedstead from the room over the hall and £20 when she reached 21; his brother John, 3, would get £1 when he reached 21. William got a table and stools from the hall and £10 to buy himself an apprenticeship - half what Elizabeth would get, but he did not have to wait until he was 21. The will includes a caveat giving Elizabeth's £20 to William if she did not live to 21; maybe she too caught the plague -

though there are no records of her death or burial. All William sen.'s goods and chattels went to his wife.

William sen. had bought the land off West Street from a Chris Westbrook in 1661, just after the Restoration. Shortly after his death, the Fareham manorial fine books show Ann transferred ownership from her husband's estate and sold them to a Thomas Penford to raise the cash to settle the legacies and pay for her husband's funeral. William jun. clearly did not inherit significant wealth from his parents.

At this point in our story it is possible to address another statement from Gregory's *History* - that William Price sen. "could only make a mark" as signature to his will. The supposed evidence for this is the fact that he dictated his will, but of course we know he did so in haste and "sicke in body", dying from the plague. He was probably too weak to sign, or perhaps his friends did not want him to touch the will because of the risk of infection - the mark on the will is that of Edward Whittinge, a witness, not William Price.

3.4   The fate of the cooperage

William dictated his will in a moment of crisis in the absence of legal advice and with no time to consider. Either might have helped him avoid the terrible mistake he made, from his son's viewpoint. 56 years later, William jun. himself left some property to a mother and her son with the words: *"I give and bequeath unto Mary Enon the wife of Thomas Enon for and during the Terme of her naturall life And after her decease I give and bequeath the said Messuages or Tenements and premyses to Thomas Enon their Son and his heires for ever"*. This meant that the mother got a lifetime trust in the property, but ownership would continue to the male heirs. However, William sen. simply left the residue of his estate to his wife Ann, and no doubt he expected her to pass it on to their children. While Ann remained a single widow, according to the customs of the manor that would happen. Were she to remarry, all her property would transfer to her new husband. What happened on her death would then be determined by his will or failing that the rules of intestacy applied to him. In either case, his relatives would likely get precedence over William's children.

Unfortunately, widow Ann Price disappears from the records, so we cannot tell what happened to the cooperage. Frank Gregory suggested the Price family fell on hard times after William's death, influencing William jun.'s decision to include the poor widows of the parish in his will, but that does not easily fit with the relative wealth of the Price family.

One possible though unlikely resolution is that Ann Price was born Ann Cortnell, who appears later in the story as marrying John Price sen. in 1670, described later in *John, son of John Price, and the Fareham cooper's shop* on page 47. This would mean that John Price jun., baptised in April 1674, would inherit the coopering business, and we know he was a cooper.

4 William Price junior, timber merchant of Fareham

In the name of God Amen the Twenty Fourth day of August in the yeare of our Lord One Thousand Seaven hundred and Twenty one, And in the Eighth yeare of his Majesties reigne etc. I William Price of the parish of Fareham in the County of Southampton Timber Merchant being aged and weak in Body, but of Sound and perfect mind memory and understanding Doe make publish and declare this my Last will and Testament

Like his father, William Price jun. left no known direct records of his life. As far as we know he left us nothing in writing apart from his signature to his will and his seal. There are no portraits or statues or even a description. A picture used to hang in a pub in West Street, Fareham, but there is record neither of the picture nor its provenance. Most likely it is a picture of an American William Price from about a century later, or even a Canadian timber merchant of the same name but nearly two centuries later! Even the Price's School lion badge is probably from the seal of a completely different William Price (see *The Price's School badge* in Appendix D on page 113).

Fareham's parish records cover his birth, baptism and death. While copies of his will exist, the estate inventory produced after his death is missing. Portsmouth Navy dockyard records several contracts with Mr Price of Fareham, and The National Archives contain records of legal cases involving him or his heirs. His family tree appears on page 7.

4.1   William Price junior's timeline

	1651	William's baptism in St Peter and St Paul's
Charles II takes throne after the Restoration of the Monarchy	1660	
	1661	Father buys some land off West Street in Fareham
	1665	Father dies as the Plague passes through Fareham
Great Fire of London	1666	
	1666–1673	Apprenticeship
Dutch cede New York to the English	1674	Marries Mary Sewatt of Bishop's Waltham
James II takes throne	1685	
Newton's *Principia Mathematica* published in Latin	1687	
William of Orange takes throne in the "Glorious Revolution"	1689	
William III defeats Irish and French in the Battle of the Boyne	1690	
	1690–1707	Contracts with Portsmouth Navy dockyard for timber
Bank of England founded	1694	
Queen Anne takes throne	1702	
Gibraltar captured from the Spanish	1704	
George I takes throne	1714	Buys land in Fareham, "Butterwick"
	1716	Buys land in Crockerhill, Fareham

	1716– 1720	Fareham borough court bailiff
	1718	Wife Mary dies
	1720	Buys land in Elson
	1721	Signs will
	1725	Death and burial in St Peter and St Paul's
George II takes throne	1727	Attorney General v. Deborah Price et al. heard in Chancery
Newton's *Principia Mathematica* published in English	1729	

4.2 Early life

We have only two records about William from his baptism to the first mention of him supplying timber to Portsmouth dockyard in 1690: the first is in his father's will in 1665 and the second the parish record of his marriage to Mary Sewatt in 1674. As with his father, we must look to history to provide a context for his life.

He spent his childhood under the Parliamentarians' Commonwealth until the restoration of Charles II to the monarchy in 1660. The Earls of Southampton reappear as the 4th, Thomas Wriothesley, becomes Lord High Treasurer. One of Wriothesley's daughters married Viscount Camden, who appears later in William's story as owner of some Titchfield estates selling timber. Samuel Pepys, who becomes clerk to the Navy Board, starts his famous diary. He is closely involved with Portsmouth Navy dockyard, as is King Charles, both of them visiting several times. The King was knowledgeable and enthusiastic in both scientific and naval matters, and gave the Royal Society its charter. He had personal discussions with the master shipwrights of the various naval dockyards, and ensured funding for naval projects that would later influence William Price's life.

As already discussed, in 1665 the Great Plague of London killed a significant part of the population not only there but also in other towns, including Southampton, Portsmouth and Fareham. It would have been a fearful time, and most Christians viewed it as an act of God, retribution for a lack of religious adherence. His father's death may well have persuaded William jun. to leave a bequest to start a charity school when he drew up his will 56 years later. Robert Hooke of Freshwater, Isle of Wight, a founder member of the Royal Society, published his "Micrographia" and is first to apply the term "cell" in the biological sense in 1665. Ironically, discoveries like this would later provide the scientific basis to understand plague.

4.3   Apprenticeship

I give and bequeath unto my Sonne William Price the some of Ten pounds for to bind him Apprentice — William Price sen.'s will.

William jun. inherited £10 to buy himself an apprenticeship, which he probably started in 1666. We know he married in 1674, and the law prohibited marriage while an apprentice, so a 7-year apprenticeship fits neatly between 1666 and 1673. Historically, apprentices would become "journeymen"(that is to say, paid by the day for their work, from the French *jour* - day) in their craft when their indenture finished. With more time and the approval of their peers, often after making a "master piece" to demonstrate their skill, they could call themselves master craftsmen and take their own apprentices. In practice by the start of the 18th century apprentices could move into different trades on finishing their indenture; the indenture certificate was beginning to be seen as a general qualification.

William could have taken an apprenticeship in a range of trades; his mother would presumably have hoped he would continue or develop the family business, so cooper, joiner, cabinetmaker, or shipwright might be suitable. As he did not become a cooper, perhaps his apprenticeship was in another trade. Given his later business with Portsmouth dockyard, he may have been indentured to a carpenter or shipwright.

The Worshipful Company of Shipwrights records:

The shipwright was a recognized craftsman, quite distinct from the house-carpenter, and shipwrights guilds existed in many places, notably Rotherhithe, Deptford and Portsmouth. These were craft guilds, not Livery companies, and their records for the most part do not survive, but we know that normal apprenticeship regulations applied. ... In a number of cases the same men can be found working as shipwrights, selling timber to the yard and providing victuals. – from *The Social History of English Seamen 1485-1649* "The English Maritime Community, 1500-1650" David Loades (2012).

No doubt the apprenticeship rules of probity and sobriety applied to dockyard servants, but boys will be boys: *"The anointing of ratts and putting fire to them is of dangerous consequence, especially in this Towne, where there are Magazeens of Powder."*– Portsmouth court presentment mentioned in *A History of Hampshire*, Thomas William Shore (1892).

The lack of a record of William as a Portsmouth dockyard servant (their term for apprentice) implies he was not an apprentice there. The story of Thomas Enon, recounted later, suggests William could have been an apprentice in Chatham dockyard, but again records there do not support this.

Richard I gave Winchester's Merchants' Guild a charter in 1190, and later Henry III granted Portsmouth a charter in 1255 and the next year allowed a Merchants' Guild, with its charter updated in 1627 by Charles I. In theory one of these guilds would require William to be a member if he were to sell timber to the Navy. Like the Shipwrights' Guild, the Merchants' appear to leave no records; again we are in the dark.

William sen.'s will mentions only a little land, and that was sold to pay his bequests. It does not seem enough to start William jun. on his career to wealthy timber merchant. The lack of records might, of course, reflect some greater change in William's life. The aforementioned Robert Hooke FRS left the Isle of Wight with £40 to buy an apprenticeship, and went to London. In a later discussion we will meet a distant relative of William's, John Price, indentured to a London ironmonger. Maybe William did likewise; there were many William Prices in London at the right time.

The Oxfords of Alverstoke

William sen. must have had contacts in the timber trade to provide his oak for barrels, perhaps with William Oxford (or Noxon or Hoxon) of Alverstoke, a shipwright and timber merchant. An article in *Gosport Records* No.12, "Weevil : Before the Royal Clarence Yard" *G.H. Williams* (1976) describes a brewery supplying the Navy, run by a John Player. This was in an area known as Weevil or Weovil, just across the inlet from what became Priddy's Hard in Elson (land that William would later own, see page 74), and contained a brew-house and notably a cooperage.

In 1673, John Player and William Oxford were partners in a contract to supply the Navy with the timber from 470 oak trees at a price of about £1,200 [TNA SP 46/137/799]. Player died in 1685, and left all his property to his kinsman Henry Player. The Players made a lot of money from the Navy, and later Henry built a large mansion, "Weevil House" on the site.

William Oxford had two sons, John and Thomas, in the same trades. Thomas had several contracts with both Portsmouth and Plymouth Navy dockyards for timber from Southwick Park. William Price jun. left a legacy to "William the son of John Oxford", so he must have been a friend or associate. (See *William son of John Oxford* on page 56 for more details.)

Here we have a cooperage, timber merchant and shipwright supplying the Navy, run by a family known to William and adjacent to land that he would later buy. While not proof that this is where he spent his apprenticeship, it strongly suggests it.

4.4   Marriage

William married Mary Sewatt of Bishop's Waltham in 1674. That area had many Sewatts (or Sewets, or Suatts, or Sewards; the name had many ways of spelling; Suet, in particular, is a fat lot of use). Mary, baptised in 1649, was the child of Henry Sewet, yeoman farmer of Hoe, Bishop's Waltham and Ursula Allen, with sisters Alice, Ursula, Anne, Frances, and Mary, and brothers John, Henry and Richard. Henry's will [HRO 1675P/31] written in 1673 shows he was moderately wealthy but not rich;

Wife Mary Sewatt

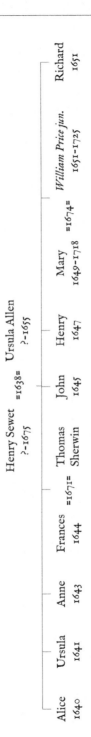

Henry Sewet   =1638=   Ursula Allen
?–1675   ?–1655

Alice   Ursula   Anne   Frances =1671= Thomas   John   Henry   Mary   =1674= William Price jun.   Richard
1640   1641   1643   1644   Sherwin   1645   1647   1649–1718   1651–1725   1651

he left his wife £40, daughters Alice and Mary 20 shillings each, and made his son John his executor and left him the residue. Their family tree is shown on the preceding page. His wife Ursula died in 1655, and a year later, Henry married Elizabeth Asten (née Loufe).

William clearly did not gain significant wealth from his wife. (The present-day Suetts Farm and Suetts Lane in Hoe, Bishop's Waltham, are almost certainly the land owned by Henry and his relatives.)

4.5 William Price junior's house

The Charity School and Master's house; [HRO 125M84/263]

William jun.'s will leaves his house on West Street to be the first Charity School building. If the picture above is accurate, his house was considerably humbler than Henry Player's mansion in Weevil. There seems to be more profit in beer than timber. The school was on the site currently occupied by NatWest Bank, now marked with a blue plaque.

The sketch above comes from a site plan in the Hampshire Record Office; as it says "present School Master's House", it was probably drawn before the school's replacement with a new building about 1845. By then the school building was in desperate need of repair; the sketch shows a wonky chimney and possibly a collapsing roof.

The proximity of this house on West Street to the field of 3 acres of barley mentioned in the inventory of his father's will suggests that it was the family home from William sen.'s time. The hearth tax records put the latter in Cams Oysell, but it is not too clear exactly where that was. The presence of today's Cams Alders recreation ground to the south-west of that site suggests the Cams name applied to quite a large part of Fareham.

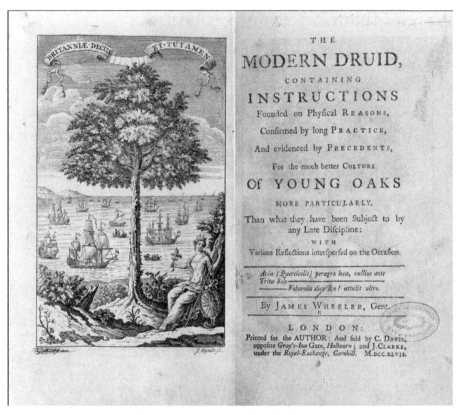

Frontispiece to *The Modern Druid* James Wheeler (1747)

4.6   The timber trade

> *... William Price late of the parish of Fareham Timber Merchant bring seized of a considerable reall Estate & possessed of a personal Estate of a Great value ...* — Chancery Court Roll [TNA C 11/1012/2]

We have already encountered timber being carried from Titchfield to Fareham to be floated down or loaded onto boats to carry it to Gosport and Portsmouth. 1666 is famously the year of the Great Fire of London, destroying 15% of London's housing and many major public buildings. That lead to a significant increase in demand for building timber over the period of William's apprenticeship. On top of this the Royal Navy's

ever-growing demand for timber was impacting supply across the world
- reflected in prices nearly doubling. Perhaps William could see which
way the wind was blowing, and took the suggested apprenticeship with
a timber merchant. If so, he chose the ideal moment.

The Great Ships programmes

While we like to believe Britannia rules the waves, it did not always go
our way. Several skirmishes during the Anglo-Dutch wars of 1652-1674
were fought close to mainland England, culminating in a raid on the
Medway in June 1667. Four capital ships were sunk, the Navy's most
significant defeat in home waters. Samuel Pepys noted in his diary:

> *All our hearts do now ake; for the newes is true, that the Dutch have
> broke the chaine and burned our ships, and particularly "The Royal
> Charles", other particulars I know not, but most sad to be sure. And,
> the truth is, I do fear so much that the whole kingdom is undone, that
> I do this night resolve to study with my father and wife what to do
> with the little that I have in money by me. ... The Dutch fleete are
> in great squadrons everywhere still about Harwich, and were lately
> at Portsmouth; and the last letters say at Plymouth, and now gone to
> Dartmouth.*

In 1675 Pepys reported to the House of Commons on shipbuilding
abroad which threatened English naval supremacy. He estimated that
the Navy would need to build over thirty "great ships" of the third to
first rate (that is, carrying from 60 to 100 guns). After much debate the
Commons in 1677 approved *"An Act for raising the Summe of Five hundred eighty foure thousand nine hundred seaventy eight pounds two shillings and
two pence halfe-penny for the speedy building Thirty Shipps of Warr"*, gener-
ally known as "The Thirty Great Ships Programme". (The accuracy
in £584,978 2s 2½d is impressive. According to the Band of England,
with inflation that is around £150m at today's prices.) The project ran
for about 10 years, and built one first-, nine second-, and 20 third-rate
ships of the line. Each ship's construction is estimated to have required
2,000-4,000 oak trees, (each about 100 years old), so 30 ships required

something like 100,000 trees. To add to this, ships required extensive refits every 5 to 10 years, more frequently if they went to war.

At a meeting of the Admiralty Commission 22nd March 1677 Charles II suggested that the Navy Board should talk to timber merchants about buying their timber, advertise in the London Gazette, write to the gentry, and invite tenders for naval commodities at the Exchange and the Custom House. Dockyard purveyors forwarded lists of both the landed gentry and timber merchants to the Navy Board and details of surveys that they carried out, as well as the dates when timber would be felled.

No sooner than the Thirty Ships programme finished, parliament approved the "Twenty Seven Great Ships" program running from 1688 to 1697, covering the first half of the period in which records show William Price contracted to provide timber to the Navy dockyard. These programmes required felling across vast areas of forest. Estimates for managed forest production range from 22 to 50 oak trees per acre, so these two programs would have cleared a century's growth from between 4,000 and 8,000 acres of oak alone.

The Navy dockyard took timber from across the south of England and further abroad (especially pine from the Baltic and North America). Local sources include, not surprisingly, Titchfield and Fareham Parks, the Forest of Bere near Wickham and Southwick Park. The dockyard's surveyor visited the forests to approve the timber. One such visit ended in tragedy - in 1678 Daniel Furzer, Master Shipwright of Portsmouth, gave orders to Richard Levermore to go to the Isle of Wight to view timber, but he was drowned getting out of the boat.

William Price's timber trade with Portsmouth Dockyard

The National Archives document series [TNA ADM 106] contain the Navy Board letters, mostly written by the Commissioners of the Royal Dockyards. Those for Portsmouth include a dozen memoranda in the period 1690-1707, each recording one "contract with Mr Price" for oak or timber. These provide the firm evidence that William Price of Fareham's timber trade was with the Navy.

Most likely William dealt in timber from other landowners. He started acquiring his own estate later. and the 150 acres bequeathed to his charity would have produced oak sufficient for just one or two ships. The Navy preferred small trades to keep prices down, and always dealt though merchants (who had the skills and knowledge to assess timber's suitability for Navy purposes) rather than directly with the landowner. (Much later attempts by the Navy to cut out the middle-man were reckoned a disaster, as the Navy Board's officers had no experience in evaluating the worth of uncut timber or trees, nor in negotiating with landowners.)

Estate owners involved in the timber trade include Lord Powerscourt (an Irish baron owning part of Bere forest), Colonel Norton of Southwick Park (whose ancestor we met in Titchfield commanding the men of Norton's Horse in the Civil War) and Wriothesley Baptist Noel, 3rd Viscount Campden of Titchfield (named after his mother's family, the Wriothesleys, Earls of Southampton). Timber merchants include William Price of course, Peter Haslar, Thomas Oxford, William Oxford, John Smith, Richard Franklin, Gilbert Jackson, Edward Benson and Ellis & Reeves.

While several dockyard memoranda mentioning timber contracts with Mr Price of Fareham survive, there are no actual contracts. A similar contract with William Oxford for timber for the 30 ships program says:

> *June 24 1678*
> *Contracted the day and yeare above said …*
> *Jno. Kempthorne Kt. one of the Com's of His Ma'ty Navy*
> *for and on the behalfe of his Ma'ty by mee Wm. Oxford*
> *of Gosport in the County of South'ton and I doe hereby*
> *oblige my selfe to deliver into his Ma'ty Yard at Portsm.*
> *free of all Charge to the King within six months*
> *from the date hereof the timber here undermentioned:*
> *Viz*
> *Compass & Straight Oake Timber three hundred trees*
> *the three hundred l'ds the bodys of said trees to meet at*
> *fifty foot each, and of Knees twenty loads at the rate*
> *and price of fourty seaven shill's p' load.*

June 24: 1670   174

Contracted the day and yeare above said w[th] S[i]r
Jn[o]: Kempthorne &c: one of the Com[issione]rs of his Ma[jes]t[ie]s Navy
for and on the behaefe of his Ma[jes]ty by mee W[illia]m Oxford
of Gosport in y[e] County of Southton and I doe hereby
oblige my selfe to deliver into his Ma[jes]ty[s] yard at Ports[mouth]
free off all Charge to the King within sixmonths
from the date hereof the Timber hereundermentioned
Vizt. Compass & Streight Oake Timber three hundred trees
q[uot] three hundred & the body of said trees to meet at
ffifty foot each, and off Knees twenty loads at the rate
and price of fourty seaven shill[ings] p[er] Load.

Elme Timber one hundred and fifty loads, which
shall meet at fourty foot in a peece at the rate and
price of Thirty eight shill[ings] p[er] Load.

Ash Timber twenty Loads to meet at eighteene
ft in a peece at y[e] rate & price of fourty two shill[ings] p[er] load.
All the s[ai]d Timber shalbe well hewed in y[e] measureing
place without shakes or red rotten, sound & Merchable
every way fitt for his Ma[jes]t[ie]s Service. To bee paid for y[e]
same upon delivering every hundred loads as afores[ai]d
I am to have a bill made out for the same & assign'd
for paym[en]t out of the money appointed to bee raised
by Act of Parliam[en]t for the building xxx New
Ships for his Ma[jes]ty Witnes my hand the day &
yeare above s[ai]d &c. (Cop[i]e) W[illia]m Oxford

William Oxford contract to supply timber to the Navy
[TNA ADM 106/336/174]

> *Elme Timber one hundred and fifty loads which*
> *shall meet at fourty foot in a piece at the rate and*
> *price of thirty eight shill's p' load.*
> *Ash Timber twenty loads to meet at eighteen feet*
> *in a piece at the rate & price of fourty two shill's p' load*
> *All these Timber shall be well hewd in the measuring*
> *places without shakes or red rotten, sound & merch'able*
> *every way fitt for his Ma'ty service. To be paid for the*
> *same upon delivering every hundred loads as afors'd.*
> *I am to have a bill made out for the same & assigned*
> *for paym't out of the Money appointed to be raised*
> *by Act of Parliam't for the building 30 New*
> *Ships for his Ma'ty. Witness my hand the day &*
> *date above. Copied Wm. Oxford*

(Compass timber is curved; knees are naturally bent pieces that buttress the join between deck and hull; shakes and red rot are timber defects. The total comes to £1,079 - around £250,000 today. How William Oxford transported 50 ft lengths of oak is not mentioned!)

The Great Storm of 1703

William Price's adult life could be said to encompass 'apocalyptic' disasters - Plague, Fire and War have already made their appearance. And in 1703, Tempest took the stage. The Great Storm hit England and Wales on the 26th November. The resulting floods in the Somerset Levels took hundreds of civilian lives, but it also hit close to William's home and trade. The Navy suffered heavily; the storm wrecked 13 ships and drowned 1,500 or more seamen. The worst impact was at the Goodwin Sands, where ships would anchor outside the Thames while waiting for a favourable wind. In this instance, the winds could not be more unfavourable. The damage reached Portsmouth - two ships, the *Newcastle* and *Vesuvius* moored at Spithead, were blown away and sank with the loss of 193 lives. Daniel Defoe's report of the storm says:

> *... And as for other trees, there has been a great destruction made*
> *of them in many places by this storm. Several were blown down at*

> *Hampton Court, and three thousand brave oaks at least, but in one*
> *principal part of the forest of Dean, belonging to his Majesty. ...*
> *And so high the winds blew for near a fortnight, that no ships stirred*
> *out of harbour; and all the vessels, great or small, that were out at*
> *sea, made for some port or other for shelter. ... At Portsmouth and*
> *Cowes, there lay three fleets ... in all 300 sail, great and small. ...*
> *Portsmouth, Plymouth, Weymouth, and most of our seaport towns*
> *looked as it they had been bombarded, and the damage of them is not*
> *easily computed.*

A year later, a note in the dockyard's papers [TNA ADM 106/585/2]
describes a surveyor's three-day trip to the New Forest to see the timber
blown down there. (Probably unconnected, another note on the same
piece of paper mentions *"Contracts I have made with Mess's Dav'd and*
Jonath'n Bone & W'm Price for Oake Timber".) The storm thus created both
supply of and demand for timber!

4.7   Guilds, courts and William Price, bailiff

Being a merchant brought rights and incurred obligations, all part of the
system of manorial courts that ran England from ancient times. Henry
III gave Portsmouth a Merchants' Guild charter in 1256. Merchants'
guilds enforced monopolies on trades within the borough. Merchants
paid fees to be allowed to open shops (for example, [HRO 97M81/4/1]
records such a payment in Romsey in 1634); in 1693 a man in Winchester
is charged with trading as a draper but neither being a free man of the
Guild Merchant of the city nor having served 7 years apprenticeship
[HRO Q25/2/38/1]. But the situation was evolving, and the guilds' power
was weakening.

     The *Victoria County History* Volume 3 "A History of the County of
Hampshire" (1908) tells us Fareham was a borough owned by the bishops
of Winchester, so its merchants would have incurred similar obligations.
Some history books suggest the merchants' guild was synonymous with
or evolved into the manorial court running a borough. However, in a
court action in 1705 "Wilton v. Wilkes", Winchester's mayor tried to
prevent Wilkes from carrying on his trade, alleging a custom that no one

should pursue his occupation unless a member of the guild-merchant. The judges said *"the words 'gilda mercatoria' signify a corporation, but what it signifies in this declaration nobody knows"*, and threw the case out saying *"it is unreasonable to restrain them from exercising their trades within this place"*.

The first record of a borough court in Fareham is in 1337, and from that date the courts were held almost continuously until 1729. A bailiff elected in the borough court governed the town. Thus in modern terms the bailiff was partly Fareham borough's executive officer, rather than just a legally-empowered debt collector as today. The election was not a public affair; only court members could vote or stand. Certainly there was a massive overlap between the merchants and those eligible to be part of the court.

William Price is elected Fareham's bailiff from 1716 to 1720. James Blakley, a mercer from Bishop's Waltham, is elected for 1723-1724; he is a witness to William's will. He is followed by Barton Reeves in 1724, one of the churchwardens charged with running the charity in the will. The same names appear in various circumstances: the list of voters in the 1713 parliamentary election includes Barton Reeves, Richard Lee, Daniel Waller and William Price. The family names of landowners of Hampshire include several names that have already appeared or will appear below: Baxter, Blakley, Eire or Eyre, Greengo, Haslar, Mooring, Norton, Rolfe, Edale, Waller and Woolgar. William was clearly part of Fareham's merchant, court and land-owning coterie.

4.8 The last years of William's life

After his period as bailiff, and after purchasing the various lands in his estate, at the age of 70 in 1721, he writes his last will and testament to found his charity school. The will is the last record of William's life. There remains only that of his burial in St Peter and St Paul's churchyard on the 3rd June 1725. It was likely a well-attended affair, with his merchant friends, many cousins, and his acquaintances from the church.

5 Fareham life at the start of the 18th century

Like his father, William jun. lived in "interesting" times. England was involved in seven wars covering more than half of the 60 years between his father's death and his own. Though the start of the Enlightenment, superstition was still rife: at her burial in 1683, a Kate Hunt of nearby Curdridge was described as a witch, maybe another reason why William wanted to start a Christian school for the poor. While Newton's *Principia*

18th Century West Street, Fareham
from a sketch by G.S. Shepherd

Mathematica was published in 1687, that was in Latin; the first English translation was only printed in 1729. The introduction of science into mechanics was yet to come: the only powered engines were the wind- and water-mill, and their design had not changed significantly for centuries.

5.1   Travel and Transport

William probably rode a horse for visits to his timber sources, but he would surely prefer water transport if possible. There is a long history of travel by "wherry" across Portsmouth harbour, a fairly flat rowing boat carrying up to 8 passengers with a long overhanging prow so they could step ashore. *The Portsmouth Harbour Story* by Burton and Musselwhite (2000) says:

> *Although crossing the harbour in rough weather in a small rowing boat was hazardous to say the least, it was infinitely preferable - and safer! - than the long dangerous journey round to Portsmouth by land on almost non-existent roads with extensive patches of marshland. Here pirates and highwaymen lurked ... There is enough evidence to suggest that a ferry service between Portsmouth and Gosport was operational from some time in the sixteenth century.*

They report that in 1602 the fares were 1d to Portsmouth, 1/2d back to Gosport, and that in 1809 Gosport council imposed a table of fares: Fareham was 4 shillings and across the harbour to Portsmouth was 6d. Possibly the dockyard would send a Navy boat if William was visiting his customer.

Fareham had a weekly cattle market just outside William's house. West Street would have been filthy and smelly from the animals' dung. There was, of course, no street lighting - houses were lit only by tallow tapers for the poor, wax candles for the rich. The "Little Ice Age" affected the climate and agricultural production; in 1684, dockyard papers record *"The men can travel from ship to ship, go ashore and up to Fareham on the ice"*, so the harbour had frozen.

Some features of modern life had spread from London - at least to Portsmouth: document [S3/B/189] in the History Centre tells us the port had six coffee houses in 1715, and as the seventeenth century saw the rise of the one-page "pamphlet", there was plenty to talk about. ...

5.2 Crime

Titchfield A History by the Titchfield History Society (1982) records:

> *In the 1760s the village was plagued by a gang who were robbing travellers on the highway from Fareham. The gang turned out to be five Titchfield men lead by a certain John Martin, a labourer.*

A gang of black-face poachers, the "Waltham Blacks" took deer from various parks, including (Bishop's) Waltham Chase during 1721-1723. The story may have been distorted by political viewpoints: few if any of the gang came from Bishop's Waltham (several came from Portsmouth), and depending on who you read they might have been common criminals, smugglers, freedom fighters or part of an aborted Jacobite uprising. What is undeniable is their activities provoked the 1723 "Waltham Black Act", a harsh law which made the maximum punishment for many offences death or transportation. A pamphlet *The History of The Blacks of Waltham in Hampshire,* possibly by Daniel Defoe, commented *"Most of the Prisoners were poor illiterate Creatures ..."*, and said they were *"ignorant of all spiritual matters"*, which would confirm William's view of the need for educating the poor.

While Fareham was becoming an up-market area favoured by naval officers for their homes, Gosport had developed a reputation for more down-to-earth facilities for the recreation of the naval ratings. An article in *Gosport Records No 6*, "Six Taverns in the Town" H.T. Rogers (1973) says

> *Women outnumbered the men by about three to two and as one old writer delicately put it in 1803 'at Gosport the Nymphs of the Sea and the Oceanides and Nereides of South Street and Rimes Alley form no inconsiderable portion of their number.' Add to this nearly seventy alehouses, three coach-houses, two theatres ... you get some idea of the busy scene. The main centre of activity was on Gosport Beach. Several hundred watermen plied for hire across the harbour and to the Royal Navy at Spithead.*

Forgery was a significant concern and severely treated. Deacon William Price the silversmith, of whom we write later, came across forged coins: Portsmouth Quarter Sessions record [S3/90/80] says a James Stimp tried to sell 30 foreign gold coins to William, whose suspicions were aroused and who therefore performed a chemical test. Stimp was sentenced to seven years transportation. Thomas Enon, another subject of a later section, accuses someone of passing him a forged coin in his change.

Then there was corruption. The Navy dockyard seems to have attracted people with a casual acquaintance with legal or moral behaviour. The Dockyard Historical Trust tells us that by 1785, the Dockyard porter was to ensure *"no persons to pass out of the Dock Gate with great coats, large trousers or any other dress that may conceal stores of any kind. No trousers are to be used by the labourers employed in the Storehouses and if anyone persists in such a custom he is to be discharged from the Yard."* Custom allowed carpenters to take wood "chips" out of the dockyard for their own use; abuse of this perk meant that "chips" could be no longer than 3 foot! The Historical Trust says that this lead to much of the woodwork (windows, furniture etc.) in the local houses being from wood of just 3 foot in length. Not that corruption was limited to the labourers: Samuel Pepys accepted rewards and gifts in return for favourable contracts, though he claimed he never allowed them to sway his judgment or influence contracts against the Navy's interest, and was quick to condemn corruption in others.

The behaviour of the Navy's master shipwrights might raise a modern eyebrow, as exemplified by one tale from *The Master Shipwright's Secrets*, Richard Ensor (2020) of the highly-respected master shipwright who was asked to assess the cost of repairing one of the King's warships. He produced a figure around a thousand pounds for replacing a few planks below the waterline. The process involved "heeling" the ship by removing heavy fittings (particularly guns) and tying its masts to a hulk to expose the hull on one side down to the keel. Having done so, and having removed a few timbers, he announced the ship needed much more timber replacing, doubling his estimate, and requiring a dry dock. Further work there apparently exposed more rot and damage, doubling the estimate again. When the King visited Deptford, he was horrified to see just the keel and some frames remaining and the ship being virtually rebuilt from scratch.

5.3   Finance

While trying to find details of the mortgage that William provided to "John Price son of John Price" - see below - it became apparent that they were very common then, as shown in the Hampshire Record Office's book *An abstract of all mortgages for 1677-1699* [HRO 11M59/C7/1/2/1]. Unlike modern times, they were not with banks or societies, but with individuals often related to the borrower, and mostly for short terms around three to five years. A surprising number, perhaps 25-30%, were provided by women - possibly rich widows.

The early 18th century had a surprisingly sophisticated financial market. The government had been raising funds to support the country's wars by organising national lotteries (see page 76) which offered annuities as prizes, and later winners were given the option to convert their prize to government stocks or shares in the South Sea Company. Other schemes to finance the government included the creation of the Bank of England.

From 1711, the South Sea Company began selling its shares - the place for "smart money" to be. By August 1720, its shares were trading at over £1,000. By the end of the year, the "South Sea Bubble" burst, and they were selling at just £100. Bankruptcies were supposedly rife. Whether the "South Sea Bubble" had anything to do with William Price making his will we can only wonder. *The Myths of the South Sea Bubble,* Julian Hoppit (2002), suggests that while William was likely to be aware of it, he is unlikely to be an investor or victim; it affected mainly the nobility, and then not as severely as often described.

5.4   Slavery

The South Sea Company brings us to the heinous crime to modern eyes of slavery.

The South Sea Company was formed in 1711 to reduce the cost of government debt to the Crown. Holders of maturing government bonds were given the option of converting them to Company shares (providing a high rate of interest) instead of repayment - thereby taking the liability off the government and delaying the bonds' redemption. But while the company's official business was *"trading to the South Seas and other parts of America, and for the encouragement of the Fishery"*, its main asset was a monopoly granted by Spain to supply African slaves to the islands in the South Seas and South America. Initially, this monopoly was worthless, as England was at war with Spain (Daniel Defoe commented in 1712 that the Spaniards would never be so stupid as to lose this monopoly, their most valuable asset). In 1714 the company did indeed enter the slave trade. In a later piece of financial engineering in 1719, the government offered national lottery annuity holders the option to convert them into Company shares.

It seems very unlikely William Price was involved in slavery. A devout Christian very much concerned for the poor, he surely was revolted by the idea of dealing in human beings. His will lists no assets other than land and property, so by the time of his death he owned no shares in the South Sea Company or any other company. He may earlier have held annuities in the form of prizes from or tickets in the State Lotteries run between 1710 and 1714, but the time-line on page 24 shows he converted his wealth into land and property during the period 1714 to 1721. The coincidence in dates between the South Sea Company's development and William buying land suggests if he was ever near becoming a shareholder, he took steps in the opposite direction to ensure he did not.

6 People in the will

William Price jun. left many bequests to his kinsmen and cousins as well as to the people named to be his executors and trustees, and some other people whose relationship is unstated. Some of these people left records that illuminate William's life story; others left nothing at all and cannot even be reliably identified from their names alone. This chapter expands on those that left the most relevant information. It starts with John, son of John Price, who turns out to be central to the progress of William Price's charity, but who remains a bit of an enigma.

6.1   John, son of John Price, and the Fareham cooper's shop

> *Item I doe hereby forgive and Release John Price Son of John Price of Fareham afforsaid the sume of One hundred pounds he ows me on Mortgage and all such Interest as shall be due for the same at the time of my decease. {provided the said John Price doe within Three months next after my decease acknowledge this my will by some writing under his hand & Seale to be duely made and Executed for that purpose}* — William Price jun.'s will

The text in braces in the above quote from William's will was an insertion added to the original text. Presumably either William or his lawyer thought it possible John might have justification to challenge the will's bequests, and considered it wise to force him to accept its intent.

A Chancery Court Roll [TNA C 11/1012/2] contains a line that tantalisingly says "as proven, John Price, the legal heir to William Price",

47

A woodcut of a German coopers shop by Tommaso Garzoni, 1641
from Deutsche Fotothek

and indicates that he is the "John Price son of John Price of Fareham" that had to acknowledge the will in order to be discharged from his mortgage. (This important case is discussed later in Appendix A on page 87.) Unfortunately, the Roll does not disclose the nature of this proof! William clearly anticipated John or John's heirs might challenge the will on the basis of being left comparatively little despite being his closest relative. We need to know more of this John Price.

John Price and Deborah Walter

A John Price married Deborah Walter in Portsmouth in 1695. Deborah inherited a shop from her father, Thomas Walter. Thomas's will of 1706, [HRO 1709P/094], is short, and left everything to his wife, another Deborah. He died very soon after, and the estate inventory shows he was a saddler, not a cooper. His wife's will of 1721 [HRO 1721P/65] left a bequest to their married daughter Deborah Preis, who countersigned the will with her husband John Preis. So the John and Deborah Price that eventually inherit the shop seem to be these same John and Deborah Preis. In confirmation of this, the Fareham parish register records the burial of an infant John son of John Price jun., *cooper* in 1700.

As it was illegal for him to marry until his apprenticeship was complete, John jun. was at least 21, more likely 25, in 1695. So he was born no later than 1674, more likely 1670, and this means his father was extremely unlikely to be William's younger brother John baptised in 1662 - unless the latter was born earlier about 1653, and baptised later for some reason. Such delays occurred, but are uncommon in the 17th century when a child would normally be baptised within a week or two of birth, and other records of the Price family seem timely. Furthermore, Willian sen. left Elizabeth £20 and William £10 legacies, whereas he left John just 20 shillings, so it appears John really is much younger than his siblings.

Copies of Fareham court roll records [HRO 36M72/E/T98] tell us that John and Deborah's grandson William inherited their cooper's shop in Fareham on the death in 1775 of his father, another William. The cooper's shop was a small (10 ft wide by 8 ft long) part of a larger shop owned by one Richard Cole. So while Thomas Walter's shop was a saddlers', as John jun. was a master cooper presumably he changed the premises' use. A William Price was buried in Fareham on 10th September 1774 aged 72, and therefore born about 1702, and William Price, cooper of Fareham, married Sarah Pasford of Titchfield on 30th September 1730. (An indenture of a John Price to a John Butcher, Ironmonger of London in 1753 says his father was "William Price, cooper of Fareham"; this John Price would have been born about 1737, and so another member of this family.)

At this point we suddenly and unexpectedly meet some corroboration, a rarity in the history of William Price, found by Professor Michael Duffy of Exeter University, an Old Pricean.

Deacon William Price of Portsea

Mr Price's great-grandfather was a very godly man, who lived at Fareham. On account of his having embraced the principles of the Baptists, his father, a wealthy man, disinherited him and left his money to support a school of boys and girls, who were to be clothed and educated. This charity (which it is understood has been much abused) is known in Fareham as Price's School. – Joseph Ivimey

The History of Price's School F.E.C. Gregory (1971) mentions a rumour in a pamphlet in 1876 quoted by W. Dumerque, chairman of the trustees, that the founder was annoyed at some relatives becoming Dissenters. The story quoted above appears in *A History of the English Baptists* Volume 4 by Joseph Ivimey (1830); it concerns Ivimey's wife's former husband, yet another William Price, deacon of the St Thomas's Street Baptist chapel in Portsea. The *Dictionary of National Biography* confirms that Joseph Ivimey married Ann Price (née Spence), a widow, in 1808.

Ivimey says this William Price, who died in September 1794, was "a respectable cutler and silversmith". The Hampshire Directory for 1784 lists William Price, Cutler in Campden Alley, Portsmouth Common. He was probably the William Price apprenticed to a James Salt, Master Cutler of Gosport in 1775, which means he was born around 1761. At this time Baptists did not record births and baptisms in any register, and no records corresponding to his birth can be found.

Ivimey says William became a member of the Baptist chapel about the age of 24. St Mary's Portsea register shows William Price and Ann Spencer married on 16th January 1786. As the law required proof of baptism before allowing marriage, Baptists often had their baptism recorded shortly before their wedding. Further research finds Ann Spencer baptised 8th March 1767 at St Mary's Portsea and buried (as Ann Ivimey) in 1829. As for his father, there's a burial record for a Baptist William Price in Portsmouth on 4th July 1788 aged 57, which makes his birth around 1731, and that fits very well with the other dates. A William Price marries Ann Jowles or Fowles in Fareham in 1759. His will records three children, Samuel, William and Ann. It therefore seems likely that Deacon William Price was the son of the William that inherited the Fareham cooper's shop in 1775, and the great-grandson of John and Deborah Price.

John Price senior

The only John son of John Price easily identified whose birth fits the ages discussed above was baptised in 1674 in Titchfield, and a John Price married Ann Cortnell in 1670 in Titchfield. He is a good candidate for the John Price whose son John married Deborah Walter. Fareham parish register records the burial of "John Price sen'r" in 1719 which fits with all the dates so far.

The founder of Price's School had no recorded children, so despite Ann Ivimey's story, the disinheriting great-great-grandfather of the Deacon William Price born about 1761 cannot have been William jun. As explained above, Deacon William's very godly great-grandfather was John Price jun., husband of Deborah, and therefore his father was, of course, John Price sen. Putting all this and some other records from the registers together results in the family tree shown on on the next page.

John Price junior's relationship to William Price junior

John Price jun. could have been just another Price from the Titchfield or Fareham area; there were plenty of Price families from which to choose, including a John Price of Stubbington. As previously described, the

John Price and Deacon William Price

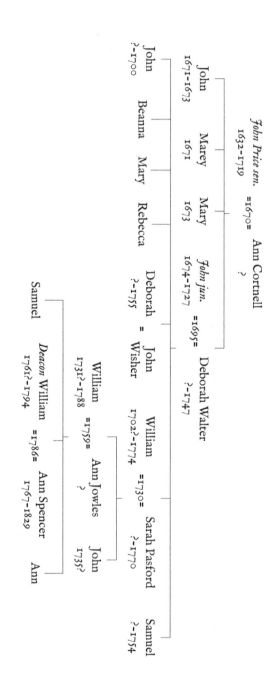

dates do not work for John to have been William's younger brother. William's legal heir would need to have been either his closest surviving cousin, or a stepfather or stepbrother. In the possible family tree starting with John and Margaret Prise, their son John was William Price sen.'s brother (see the family tree on page 7). He would have been 30 in 1632, and so it is possible his son was the John sen. that married Anne Cortnell. In that case, John sen. would be William jun.'s eldest cousin, and thus his family would indeed have been William's closest cousins.

As described in *The fate of the cooperage* on page 21, there is a small possibility that the Anne Cortnell who married John Price sen. was William Price's widow. That would be a marriage between a widow and her step-nephew, which was prohibited by the 29[th]entry *"A Woman may not marry with her Husband's brother's son"* in the *Book of Common Prayer* (1662) "Table of Affinity". This could explain a marriage under her maiden name and in a different parish, Titchfield rather than Fareham. This is purely conjecture, but it would mean that John jun. would inherit, via Ann, William sen.'s cooperage business, in turn explaining the antipathy between William jun. and John jun. later on.

John Price jun. ended up well-off. His 1727 will, [HRO 1727B/47], says:

> ... *to my Dearly beloved wife Deborah all my dwellings with the goodes chattells therein & likewise the lands lying & being at Elson for her life and after her decease to my son William Price.*
> *Item ... my son Samuel Price the sume of one hundred & twenty pounds*
> *Item ... my daughter Beanna Price the sume of sixty pounds*
> *Item ... my daughter Mary Price the sume of sixty pounds*
> *Item ... my daughter Rebecca Price the sume of sixty pounds*
> *Item ... my daughter Deborah the wife of John Wisher the sume of sixty pounds to be paid or allowed her out of the some of One hundred and ten pounds which is now due my mortgage made to me by the said John Wisher ...*

These bequests total £360, and observe that he claimed ownership of the lands at Elson. In comparison, William jun.'s cash bequests totalled just over £260 in 1721.

6.2   Peter Price senior of Fareham

The list of bequests involving Thomas Price and his sister Mary makes it likely that they are children of Peter and Elizabeth Price, most of whose family were baptised in Fareham. The Titchfield and Fareham registers provide the following possible family members (with Peter sometimes spelled as Petter or Peeter): Peter Price son of Peter Price baptised in 1643 in Fareham; children Peter and Elizabeth baptised in Fareham, then John, William, and Thomas baptised in Titchfield, and finally Robart [*sic*], Mary and another Elizabeth (the first died in infancy) baptised back in Fareham. Mary marries Thomas Briant, and Elizabeth marries John Shaw, both of whom appear in the will.

Presumably Peter sen. is a close relative of William sen., and is likely to have been born before 1620; possibly he was William sen.'s brother. He may be the Peter Price who marries Ann Knight in Titchfield in July 1642. A Peter Price Coopar dies in Titchfield in 1665; assuming that means "the Peter Price who is a cooper" rather than "Peter Cooper", the only candidate is Peter sen. This family tree appears on the facing page. Names in italics appear in the will.

Cousin Peter Price

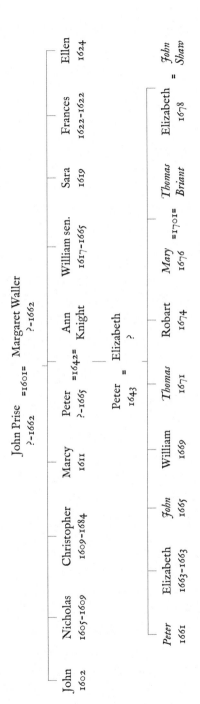

6.3   William son of John Oxford

William Price jun.'s will leaves five pounds to William the son of John Oxford. His family tree is shown on the next page. Its derivation is complex and confusing.

The wills of William Oxford [HRO 1685P/18] and Thomas Oxford [HRO 1668B/40] - the sons of William Oxford previously mentioned in *The Oxfords of Alverstoke* on page 28 - both use the surname "Oxford or Noxon", say they are brothers, shipwrights, and that they live in Alverstoke. As most people only write their wills near the end of their lives, we may assume they were born early in the 17th century.

Thomas Oxford's will mentions sister Ellenor [*sic*], wife of William Symonds. Elenor marries William Symonds in Steep in 1631, and then, as Elenor Symonds, marries William Wakeford in Petersfield in 1662 . They in turn appear as William and Eleanor Wakefield in a case in Chancery [TNA C 5/55/87] challenging the will of Jonas Noxon of Steep in 1669. Jonas Noxon was born in 1613, the son of Andrew Noxon and Elizabeth Garie of Steep. There are no records for Thomas and William Oxford or Noxon born in the early 1600s in Hampshire, but if Thomas, William and Ellenor are siblings, their presumed dates would fit with being Andrew and Elizabeth's children. Thomas Oxford marries Joane Mathew in Alverstoke in 1638, which make Thomas born around 1614.

William Oxford's will mentions his wife Sarah, his eldest son John William, and his daughter Elizabeth Missing. Elizabeth Oxford marries William Missing in Titchfield in 1669. This introduces William Noxon's family in Titchfield: Elizabeth baptised in 1649. William 1651, Ann 1653, Thomas 1657 and Mari 1661. This suggests William was born around 1625. The son William born in 1651 is presumably the John William mentioned in the will. This puts the Oxfords in Titchfield at the same time as the Prices, and John William Oxford as William Price jun.'s contemporary.

John William Oxford's son Thomas marries Hannah Clemence in 1692 in Titchfield, and they move to Southwick. It is probable this Thomas Oxford is the timber merchant from Southwick mentioned in Portsmouth dockyard records selling timber to the Navy.

John Noxon and Margaret Bettesworth marry in Steep in 1670, and have a son William in 1671 in Alverstoke. This is the only William son of

The Oxford or Noxon family tree

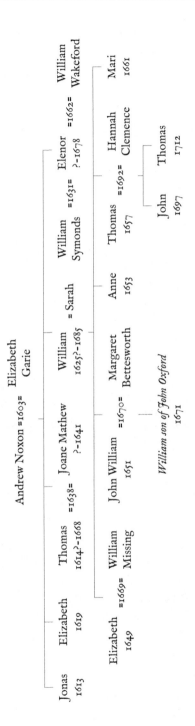

John Oxford (or Noxon) alive at the time of the will, so it appears John William Oxford is this John Noxon and their son is thus William son of John Oxford.

6.4   Thomas and Mary Enon

All those my messuages or tenements with Thappurtances scituate and being in the parish of Portsea in the Said County which I purchased of William Bragg I give and bequeath unto Mary Enon the wife of Thomas Enon for and during the Terme of her naturall life And after her decease I give and bequeath the said Messuages or Tenements and premyses to Thomas Enon their Son and his heires for ever. — the first bequest in the will.

The first bequest in a will is usually to the most important friend or relative apart from the spouse or first son and heir (who usually inherits the residue of the estate). Mary Enon and her son inherited houses and land and any rental income therefrom. William must have considered they deserved special favour above his kinsmen who appear later and got much more modest financial bequests. A subsequent clause leaves bequests to Thomas and Mary Enon's children Mary, William and Price (yes, it is also a Christian name). A search of parish registers and marriage licences turns up a Thomas Enon of Portsmouth, widower, who married Mary Bradford of Fareham, spinster, on 18th January 1712 in Rowner.

William was related to Mary Bradford. His will contains a separate large bequest *"To my cousin Mary Bradford Forty pounds"* so it seems there are two Mary Bradfords, mother and daughter, probably Mary sen. related to William (perhaps née Price or Sewett/Suett) and Mary jun. married to Thomas Enon. Yet again, there are no records to tie the Bradfords to the Prices or Sewatts.

The land in Portsea ultimately becomes Thomas Enon jun.'s property. Possibly William agreed to become godfather to his kinswoman Mary sen.'s daughter, and thus Thomas jun. became in William's mind his dearest if not nearest male heir.

A family tree for Thomas Enon appears on page 60.

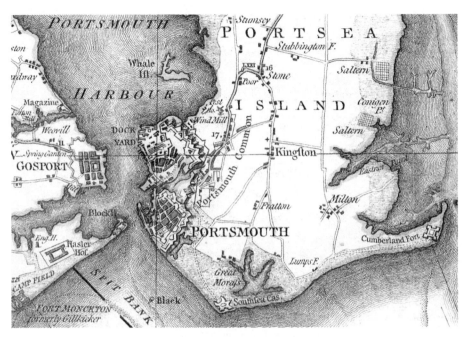

Portsea, from Milne's 1791 map
Hampshire County Museums Service.

Thomas Enon senior

Thomas Enon sen. appears only on the periphery of William Price's story, but his life illu-
minates the operation of the Portsmouth Navy
dockyard.

Enon, like Price, is a Welsh name, as is Eynon
(also Einon). The Eynon family has a long as-
sociation with shipbuilding; other Enons were
dockyard Master Carpenters, and the associ-
ation continues until the 20th Century - Green-
wich Royal Museum contains a model of John
Eynon's "Gripwell" anchor patented in 1902.
There is no way to determine whether "Enon"
and "Eynon" are simply coincidentally similar,

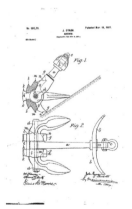

Eynon's patent
"Gripwell" anchor

or in fact the same name misspelled. The name Enon appears to suffer

Thomas and Mary Enon

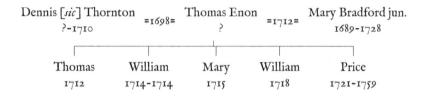

Dennis [*sic*] Thornton   Thomas Enon   Mary Bradford jun.
       ?-1710   =1698=   ?   =1712=   1689-1728

Thomas	William	Mary	William	Price
1712	1714-1714	1715	1718	1721-1759

more misspellings or transcription errors than most.

Finding Thomas Enon's origins is challenging because of the erratic spelling of his surname over the years. Findmypast.com lists Enons in the Medway towns near the Navy dockyard in Chatham: the wedding of Thomas Enon and Dennis [*sic*] Thornton in 1698 in Frindsbury near Chatham, Kent, and the baptisms of son Freeman (1699) and daughter Dennis (1701). Dennis Epion [*sic*] (presumably Denise Enon), wife of Thomas Epion, was buried there 28th Dec 1710. Further digging uncovers the baptism of Thomas son of Thomas Eson [*sic*] in Rochester in 1675, so our Thomas seems to have been firmly rooted in the area until the death of his first wife, after which he moved to Portsmouth dockyard in about 1711, probably on the Navy's orders. We also know he was a shipwright in Rochester, as he took an apprentice (Rob Butler) in March 1710. Thomas and Mary had a son, again Thomas, baptised in 1712 in Fareham, other sons William and Price, and a daughter Mary in 1715.

A Price Enon. mariner, wrote his will in 1767 while on HMS *Bonetta*, a privateer, before sailing for Florida, leaving everything to his honourable father Thomas Enon, shipwright, of the parish of Portsea. This probably isn't the Price Enon born to Thomas and Mary above, as he probably died in 1759, but quite likely one of his cousins; there seem to be several Price Enons in both Portsmouth and Gillingham to choose from! However, it appears either Thomas Enon sen. had a long life in Portsmouth, or Thomas Enon jun. also had a son Price and became a shipwright in Portsmouth.

Thomas Enon sen. was not a man to be trifled with - Portsmouth Quarter Sessions deposition [S3/63/90] of 1714 states: *"Thomas Enon*

HMS *Coronation*, sister ship to HMS *Neptune*

makes oath that within the last week John Drew gave him twenty shillings & one penny as change of Guineau given by Thomas to John who deducted five pence due to him. Further that among the money there was a Brass crown given to him by John as good silver."

HMS Neptune

The Royal Navy and Admiralty records in the National Archives contain several letters concerning Thomas Enon, carpenter, as do the records of taxes paid on apprentices' indentures. In January 1712 he was appointed the Master Carpenter of HMS *Neptune* in Portsmouth dockyard. In 1721 he was still Master Carpenter of the *Neptune*, taking another apprentice Thos. Harmsworth. His wife Mary died and is buried in 1728 in Fareham. In 1739 a Thomas Enon is Master Carpenter of HMS *Prince* living in Gillingham, where he died in 1745, but this appears to be a different Thomas.

Thomas sen. - the one living in Portsmouth - seems to have been a bit of a rascal - Quarter Sessions deposition [S3/90/80] of 1728 states *"John Marshall overseer swears that Thomas Enon shipwright refused to accept William Rawlins as a parish apprentice or his 40/- premium on the indenture counterpart"*.

A ship's Master Carpenter was responsible for its maintenance and repair either at sea or in dock. Thomas would have served a seven-year apprenticeship (or in dockyard parlance been a carpenter's "servant") before becoming a carpenter himself. With experience, he would have earned a warrant appointing him as an officer (that is, a warrant officer as distinct from a wealthy person who would have bought their commission). In the naval hierarchy of the time, warrant officers took orders from commissioned officers (who had no qualifications apart from money), and gave orders to ordinary seamen. As a naval officer, he would have been ordered from place to place as necessary, so his presence in Portsmouth or Gillingham tells us little about his family home.

HMS *Neptune* was built as part of the 1677 "Thirty Great Ships" program (described on page 33), and launched at the Navy dockyard in Deptford, London in 1683. She saw action at the Battle of Barfleur in 1692, and was later rebuilt at Blackwall yard, being relaunched in 1710 as a 90-gun "second-rate ship of the line" with a complement of 680 men. Almost immediately her crew were paid off, and she was put into reserve in Portsmouth in 1711. There, Thomas would have been responsible for keeping her in working condition so that if she was required once more she could be recommissioned for action. The *Neptune* was a major fighting ship - the biggest second-rate - so this was a significant appointment for Thomas. The dockyard payroll lists Thomas as Master Carpenter along with a Master Gunner, a Cook and a Bos'n as part of a group of just ten "Shipkeepers" rather than the full operational complement. So possibly he was not such a senior figure, though he was paid well.

Under Charles II, it was common for maimed sailors (and the wars meant there were many) to be given undemanding work in the dockyard while still on full wages, particularly as ship's cook. Maybe Thomas was injured in action and was made Master Carpenter as a sinecure.

6.5   Some other people named in the will

Not much is known about many of the people mentions in William's will. Information gleaned about the following persons illuminate some aspects of his life:

Thomas Sherwin junior was a cousin left £5 in the will. Thomas Sherwin married Frances Sewatt in Bishop's Waltham in 1671, which makes him William Price's brother-in-law. A Joan Sherwin, wife of Thomas Sherwin of Crockerhill, is granted probate after his death in 1722. He was a brick maker at the Crockerhill brickyard. Frances Sherwin dies in Wickham in 1723; perhaps she also went by the name of Joan.

Edward Sherwin was a cousin presumably closely related to Thomas. He seems to be a farmer in Wickham. He and Thomas may well be the sons of a Thomas Sherwin who dies in Wickham in 1701, aged 100!

Churchwardens

Barton Reeves was later the bailiff of Fareham.

William Greene owned land in Posbrook near Titchfield, and a 1726 sacrament certificate for him living in Bronwich, Titchfield [HRO Q25/2/28/45] describes him as a gentleman of Fareham parish. He seems to have leased Bromwich Farm from the Duke of Beaufort and Duchess of Portland, who owned Titchfield Park and supplied timber to the dockyard.

John Gringo(e) was a rich Titchfield ironmonger. In consideration of marriage portion of £1000 he obtained grants to the Manor of Hardley, Fawley and a messuage and 200 acres in Shalfleet in trust for the use of Elizabeth Gringo for her life. Peter Gringo of Wickham, cordwainer, mortgaged part of the tenement (5 low rooms and 3 upper rooms) in Wickham belonging to John Gringo, hammerman to John Woolgar, Fareham yeoman, for £23 12 sh. John Gringo of Fareham offered to buy up the scrap metal around

Portsmouth dockyard in 1728. He was also involved in salvaging a boat sunk in Portsmouth harbour.

William Bennett renewed the lease of Fareham parsonage in 1680, 1708 and again 1718. The will of a William Bennett of Fareham, Hampshire, blacksmith 1672 may identify his father. The Bennetts family had the lease of the vicarage for "three lives" and received the "greater tithes" (worth £300 in 1698) from the mid 17th century until 1840. (The *British Victoria History of Hampshire* says *"In the reign of William III, and again in that of Anne, several disputes arose between the master and brethren of St. Cross and the vicar of Fareham as to the payment of certain tithes, and evidence was brought to show that the former had no interest in any lands that had hitherto paid tithes to the vicar."* Legal dispute seems to have been feature of life for middle-class merchants of this time.) Familiar names William Bennett, William Rolfe, and Benjamion Bagiter [Benjamin Bagster] of Fareham appear in a Portsmouth dockyard memorandum in 1678 averring 2 pence per load of timber had always been the duty paid to the Fareham hoy for carriage in what seems to be an argument about the price.

Witnesses

George Huish dealt in land 1719, and was town clerk at Portsmouth in 1722. The Portsmouth History Centre has a record of a complaint from Samuel Leeke, Lord of the Manor of Portsea, mentioning him:

Memorandum August 13th 1702

Complint having been made by me to John Godwin Esq. Mayor of Portsmouth that the Boundary Post called Feltons Gibbet which was washed down about five years ago by the Sea had since been erected in a different Place to what it ought to stand, Mr Godwin attended by Mr George Huish Town Clerk, James Conver Town Serjeant, & Wm Gile, Tho's Bromfield, Thos Baker, – Cheesman, – Whiting, & Frost, Constables of the Borough afore-said met me there this day at

*one oclock when it was agreed that it should be removed to that part of
the Beach so it bringe the Muzzle of the Middle Gun on the Mount
of the Bastion near Kepple's Row in Portsmouth into a line with the
Windmill built of bricks on Portsdown near Widley Summer House,
which was determined upon to be as near as possible to the Spot where
it antiently was placed.*

B. Huish Barbara Huish, George's wife.

James Blakley a mercer and landowner of Bishop's Waltham in 1699,
also later the bailiff of Fareham.

Executor

John Woolgar A John Woolgar of Wickham left a legacy of 40 shillings
to John Price son of William Price, who was therefore William
Price jun.'s brother. William described him as "kinsman", so presumably John Woolgar sen. married either a Sewatt or a Price.

7 Land in the wills

When the Prices made their purchases, landholdings tended to comprise a patchwork of plots resulting from splits between inheritors or piecemeal sales over the centuries. Land ownership was perhaps the most fragmented at that time. Over the subsequent centuries big landowners endeavoured to buy adjacent plots, returning to larger agglomerations. The 1840 Tithe Apportionments show that tithes were due to Sir John Brocas Whalley-Smythe-Gardiner, owner of Roche Court, and the fine books show his family buying back many small plots. As a result, by then he and the Price Charity divided up a significant part of north Fareham agricultural land.

7.1 William Price senior's land

my said daughter Elizabeth is to receive out of the land which I have surrendered to my wife the Some of twenty pound

William sen. bought a couple of fields off West Street, Fareham from a Chris Westbrook in 1661. After William's death, his widow Ann sold them to a Thomas Penfold. The fine book indexes record several further transfers over the next 150 years, the last being to a Mary Jurid or Jurd in 1836. The tithe apportionments record two plots owned by Mary Jurd on West Street, about 3 acres, as shown in the map on the next page. The charity never owned this land.

As previously mentioned, the inventory for William's will after his death shows his estate included a field of three acres of barley, and it is possible this is the same field.

Price senior's land off West Street, Fareham

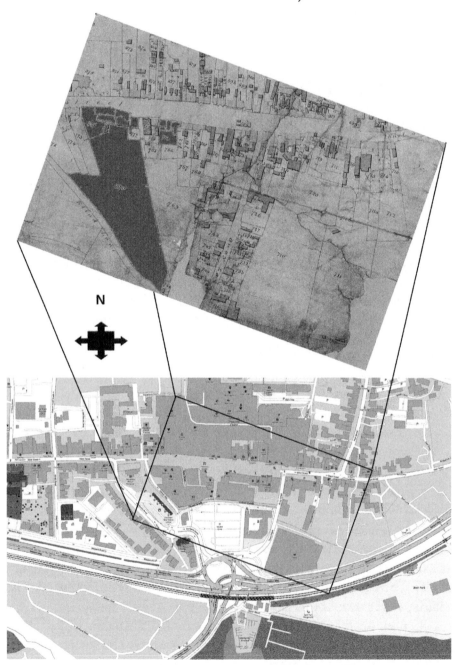

Also shown is the small plot next door but two to the east which the tithe map records as "House, Garden and School" owned by Price's Charity.

7.2   Land purchased from Mr Benjamin Bagster

William Price jun.'s will mentions *"the Land I purchased of Mr Benjamin Bagster"* as part of his charity's endowment, alongside land in Crockerhill and Elson. According to a bill in the Court of Chancery (see Appendix A on page 87), William sold this land between drafting his will and his death. Bagster appears several times on the periphery of William's story. He, or more likely his father, was a solicitor involved in land deals concerning the estate of Sir William Uvedale of Wickham 1587-1652, who incurred debts to Charles II. Uvedale had been Charles's Chancellor, charged with raising around £600,000 to finance his wars. I wonder if the King held him personally responsible for the amount, and effectively bankrupted him when he failed to collect enough from the rest of the nobility in government.

Sir William's widow Lady Victoria Carey married one Bartholomew Price of Llanspyddid, Brecknockshire. Both print books and the Internet are full of references to "Bartholomew Price of Linlithgow", but this seems to be a misreading of "Llanspyddid" in his will or marriage records. In fact the will makes it abundantly clear that Bartholomew Price was the brother of Sir Herbert Price MP of Wales, a member of the Welsh nobility. Bartholomew studied at Oxford and appears to have entered the clergy. Perhaps he was the Uvedale's family priest, and shared Lady Victoria's company in spiritual pursuits before her much older husband Sir William's demise.

There are no records of Prices in Linlithgow (nor sadly to connect Bartholomew Price's family to William Price's). The original source of this error appears to be an article in the Surrey Archaeological Society's *Collections relating to the History and Antiquities of the County, Volume 3:* "Notices of the Family of Uvedale", *Granville Leveson Gower Esq., MP* (1845) which simply states *"She re-married at St. Benets Church, Paul's Wharf, on the 14th August, 1653, Bartholomew Price, Esq., of Linlithgow"*. Unfortunately, the error propagated into *Burke's Peerage*.

There is a more mundane connection between Bartholomew and William: Bartholomew Price's will left a legacy of £5 to Benjamin Bagster, and as mentioned above, Bagster sold land to William. The Bagsters were likely involved in the sale of Uvedale's estates in Surrey and Hampshire - the latter mostly around Wickham, and including land in Crockerhill.

Of general interest, if no relevance to the Prices' story, is the fact that through his marriage to Uvedale's widow, Bartholomew Price became owner of Portchester Castle. He and Lady Victoria leased it for "three lives" to a John Antram, yeoman of Portchester for £280 in 1664, according to records in the Hampshire Record Office [HRO 4M53/K11].

7.3   Land purchased from Robert Swan

William's will also mentions land *"purchased of Robert Swan scituate within the Tything of North Fareham"* which he leaves to Peter son of Peter Price. This appears to be a field of 7½ acres just north-west of Roche Court and adjacent to William's Crockerhill estate, now just to the north side of the M27 motorway.

The chain of ownership in the fine book indexes starting from William to Peter continues with members of the previously-mentioned Ivimey family. It is therefore possible Peter was on good terms with John son of John Price, and perhaps Peter was also a Baptist.

7.4   Crockerhill

All that my Land and Estate att Crocker hill aforsaid parte of which is called by the name of Prices Land, and the other parte Lees Land with the Messuages Barnes and other Buildings and appurtenances thereunto belonging and the small purrock of Coppyhold Land containing Two acres lyeing in the midle of my said Estate att Crocker hill

This today forms part of the land still called Charity Farm situated on the A32 Wickham Road a bit north of the junction with the M27. A board

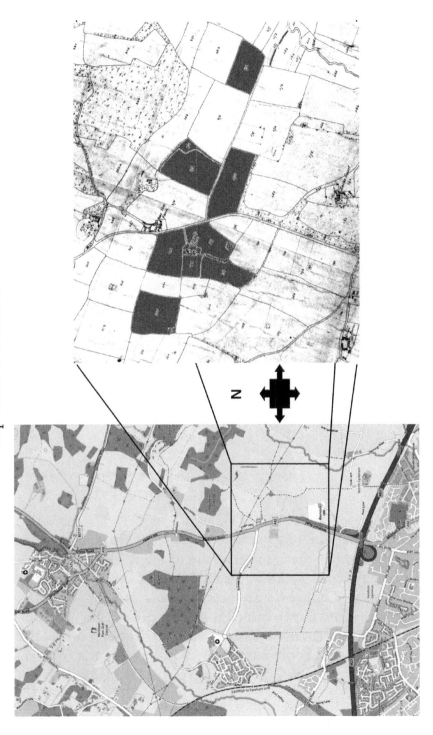

Map of land in Crockerhill

that used to adorn the wall in Price's School states that the Price's estate in Crockerhill was about 50 acres. The fine book index says William bought land from Richard Lee in 1716. See the map on the previous page. William seemed very attached to the items in the dwelling there, and said they should not be taken away. In theory, there is a house there still containing two furnaces, a clock, mirror, eight chairs and a table! Maybe the house was Thomas and Frances Sherwins', and these items were a wedding gift to his sister-in-law..

7.5   Butterwick

All those my Coppyhold Lands with Thappurtances called Butterwick with the Small Purrock thereto adjoining which I purchased of Mrs Mooring Lyeing within the Mannor of Fareham (which said Coppyhold Lands as well as the other Lands hereinafter mentioned scituate and being within the said Mannor I have surrendred to the use of my Last will and Testament) I give and bequeath unto my kinsman Thomas Price the son of Peter Price and his heires forever according to the Custom of the said Mannor, he and they paying thereout the severall Legacys

Butterwick was about 19 acres in what is now Park Lane with a rent payable to the vicar of £3 6s 6d in 1836, and was marked by Butterwick Cottages there in the 1920s. The site of the 1908-1989 Price's School was directly across Park Lane (called Puxol Lane in 1920 and earlier). The Fareham Leisure Centre occupies much of what was Butterwick. A merchant Paul Green owned it in 1756; presumably Thomas Price sold it to settle the various legacies. The charity never owned this land. The borough fine book index shows William bought it from Hannah Mooring, widow, in 1714. See the map on the facing page.

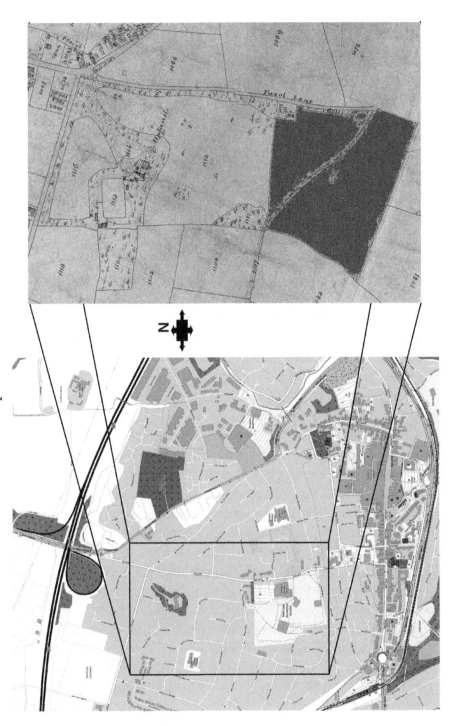

Map of Butterwick

7.6   Elson

And alsoe my Farme and Lands with Thappurtences at or near
Elson in the parish of Alverstoake in the said County, which I lately
purchased of Daniell Waller

William bought the land off Daniel Waller for £1,460 in 1720, according to the records of a 1720 Bill in Chancery "Price v. Waller" [TNA C 11/2722/15]. That is about £320,000 in 2021 prices, according to the Bank of England's calculator.

Discussed in a later bill in the Court of Chancery (1728, see Appendix A on page 87), John Price, son of John Price, inherited it on William's death and refused to convey it to the charity's trustees. The Alverstoke court roll [HRO 48M74/M1] records on 3rd September 1725 *"We present the death of Wm. Price since the last court, whereby a Relief of £2 15s 1d become due to the Lord of this Liberty. We present Jno. Price as heir at Law to part of the estate, the residue being given to the Support of a Charity School."*, and later on 16th October 1727, *"We present the Death of Jno. Price late of Fareham whereby a relief of 14s is due to the Lord of this Liberty and payable by Jno. Price son and heir at Law of the deceased."* (This seems incorrect: John Price, cooper, husband of Deborah Walter, was the one that died in 1727 and their son John died in 1700; the heir was their son William.)

In 1765, Price's Charity sold part of this land to the government Board of Ordnance for the munitions works known as Priddy's Hard and the Magazine in Gosport. It is now site of the "Explosion Museum of Naval Firepower", part of the National Museum of the Royal Navy. The 1842 Alverstoke tithe apportionment [HRO 21M65/F7/4/1] lists a total of over 108 acres of land owned by the Trustees of Price's Charity and 44 acres by the Board of Ordnance. See the map on the facing page.

The earlier Bill in Chancery concerned William Price jun.'s purchase of the lands from Daniell Waller and his wife in February 1720. Daniell may have been one of William's cousins - the possible family tree on page 7 has Margaret Waller as William's grandmother. It says that Waller reneged on the contract in the following June, and claimed William had

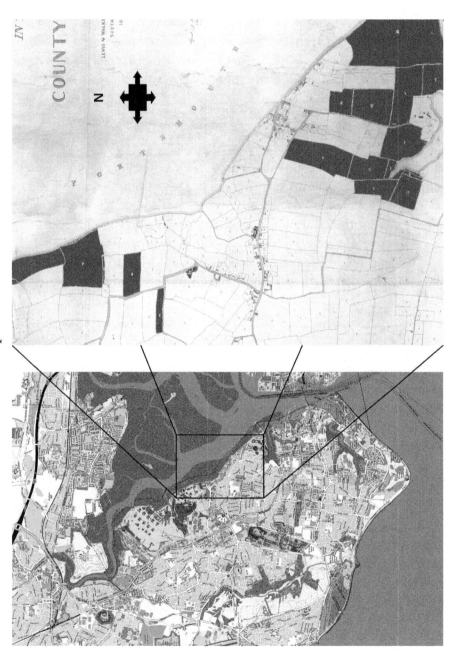

Map of lands in Elson

not paid enough - William said he was gazumped. William presumably won the case, or reached a settlement with Waller, as we know the land was conveyed to him.

There are a couple of interesting phrases in this Bill: *"your Orator should be forced to dispose of some Lottery Annuities to raise the said purchase money"*, and *"on or about the twenty seventh day of April last past a dedimus potestatem was sined out, and directed to the person therein mentioned"*.

dedimus potestatem

This Latin legal phrase means approximately "we have given the power", and is used when a court or other legal body appoints a proxy for some purpose. It was often used when someone who had to give sworn testimony before the court was unable to travel to do so. The court would give a representative a *dedimus potestatem* authorising them to receive the testimony in the person's home. Perhaps by 1720 William Price jun. was no longer in the best of health, though it might have been Daniell Waller who was unable to travel.

National lotteries

The first English national lottery was the 1694 "Million Adventure", a money-raiser for the government (at the time fighting the Nine-years war with France). 100,000 tickets costing £10 each offered prizes of 16-year annuities, the top prize being £1000 *per annum*, the bottom being £10 p.a. But that's not all - even losing tickets paid £1 p.a. for 16 years (an effective rate of interest of 6.15%).

The draw took tickets from two chests; one chest held ticket stubs from purchased tickets, the other chest a similar number of paper sheets either blank or with a prize. The drawing official took a ticket from the first chest and one from the second; if the second ticket had a prize, it was awarded to the owner of the first ticket. Losing tickets were said to have *"drawn a blank"* - the origin of this phrase. Queen Anne's government ran no less than 7 state lotteries between 1710 and 1714, bringing in over one billion pounds in modern terms, and the rate of interest in the resulting annuities ranged upwards of 4% in a time when inflation was less than 2%.

The annuities' interest meant there was a market for losing tickets, and created several other financial products based on the lottery. These included sweepstakes to share the purchase cost of a ticket across several people, and a bank that bought lottery annuities and paid a lower interest rate but for a longer term. "Creative" financial speculation is not a new invention. Thus Daniel Waller's suggestion that William Price sold some annuities could indicate anything from buying ticket that won a top prize to buying "losing" tickets - William could have been a shrewd investor rather than a lucky gambler!

8 Afterword

The William Prices, father and son, lived through turbulent times - the Civil War, the Great Plague, the Great Fire of London, the Restoration of the Monarchy - and saw significant changes that left their mark on history. Winston Churchill wrote, *"Those that fail to learn from history are doomed to repeat it."* The Prices' times bear many similarities to the early 21st century - pandemic, religious fundamentalism and intolerance, autocratic despots; we seem not to have learnt as much from history as we might.

8.1 William Price, the man

William Price left few traces apart from the Charitable Trust that bears his name, and the lasting benefits to 250 years of pupils at Price's School. The last school to bear the Price's name, a sixth-form college, closed in 1989, but the name lives on in the memories of the Society of Old Priceans.

He was generous to his relatives and friends, possibly giving his sister-in-law's family gifts for their home in Crockerhill. He granted John a mortgage and then wrote a clause into his will absolving him of the debt, and he left his Portsea estate to perhaps his God-daughter's son Thomas Enon jun. He left his land in North Fareham to his cousin Peter Price. As well as these large gifts, he made bequests totalling £260 - about £40,000 in 2021 money - to his friends, relations and in-laws.

William Price was not a vain man - his will ordered no statue or monument, and it did not even specify a name for his "charity school". He was generous, but not blind to weaknesses in others, and was a good judge of men - he realised John Price and John Woolgar's possessiveness might lead them to challenge the charitable provisions of his will, and included appropriate clauses. Notwithstanding that, he appointed Woolgar his executor. William probably employed and negotiated with many characters of men in his timber merchant days, and he learnt accordingly. He was not averse to recourse to the law when not treated fairly.

William was religious, a staunch member of the Church of England, and trusted the vicar and churchwardens of St Peter and St Paul's to set up his charity school after his death. His founding of a bluecoat charity school may have motivated by the Society for the Promotion of Christian Knowledge (see *Bluecoat schools* on page 107), the experience of his widowed mother's hardship after his father's death from plague, a belief that the catastrophes of war, plague and tempest that affected his lifetime were God's punishment for man's sinful ways, and a desire to reduce crime, superstition, ignorance and poverty.

Despite no doubt expensive legal advice and an acquaintance with the workings of the legal system, William still made fundamental mistakes in his will. He specified fixed sums for the schoolmaster's salary and similar items, making no allowance for inflation nor giving the charity trustees any means of varying them. He specified the trustees both by name - Edmund Jenkins, etc. for the fitting out of the new school, and by roles - vicar and churchwardens of St Peter and St Paul's for the trustees to run it. It seems likely these were not just parish notables, but personal friends, given their appearance in other parts of William Price's life story. He probably hoped his friends would further endow the school in their wills. Unfortunately, Edmund Jenkins died in 1725, and a new vicar Daniel Wavell replaced him. Wavell did not bother to attend the church in person, and appointed curates to run the church and its offices, and he replaced the churchwardens. This lead to the legal bill heard in Chancery (see Appendix A on page 87).

8.2   William Price and Christ's Hospital School

And in Default of performance of the severall direccions above men-
tioned according to the true intent and meaning of this my will, Then
I give and bequeath all my Estate herein before devised for the main-
tainance of the said Schoole To Christ Church Hospital in London —
the will

William was clearly very well aware of Christ Church Hospital's school
(founded in 1552, nowadays called Christ's Hospital School, and moved
from Newgate, London to Horsham) - the original bluecoat charity
school. His will leaves the money to it if his executors fail to set up the
school in Fareham. Yet there are no records linking anyone in his story
to the school. Records show that Christ's took over 100 pupils from
Hampshire before 1700, but none of the families in William's story seem
to have had children there at the right time.

A rather different possible connection is the redoubtable Samuel
Pepys. Pepys was clerk to the Navy Board 1660-73, then secretary to the
Admiralty 1673-79 and again 1684-89. He visited Portsmouth dockyard
frequently, for a time had a house there, and in 1662 he was granted the
freedom of the City.

Pepys was involved in raising funds for the foundation of the Royal
Mathematical School at Christ's Hospital in 1673, and was later a governor there. Separate from the bluecoat school, it was intended to train
40 boys in navigation for the benefit of the Navy. Perhaps he made a
public address on the subject while at the dockyard, inspiring William
to consider the need for a charity school in Fareham.

8.3   The passing of the bluecoat schools

There was one more clause in the will that may have determined the
history of Price's school: the schoolmaster was allowed to teach no other
children. Maybe this clause was to ensure the school remained true to
his intention to educate the poor. The great public schools of England
started life as charities. Today, Christ's Hospital School charges over
£39,000 per annum per pupil. Winchester College, similarly founded as

a charity school, has 70 free "scholars" and about 9 times as many pupils paying over £43,000 p.a. per pupil.

According to the *Encyclopaedia of Education* published by Pitman (1921), over 1,000 bluecoat charity schools were established by 1720. Like Price's, their small classes could not provide the breadth and depth of the state schools, and they could no longer stay true to their charity's intentions once the state started to fund general education. The vast majority of those bluecoat schools, like Price's, have vanished or been absorbed into the state system. As a counter-example, the independent Birmingham Blue Coat School gained significant endowments over its early years, and by 1939 had an income around £14,000 supporting 140 or so pupils. However, by 1954 it was considering charging fees to cover its increasing shortfall. Nowadays it has become a non-boarding preparatory school with fees around £16,000 p.a.

8.4   A story of the founder of Price's School

Despite much research, four days at The National Archives in Kew, and a dozen trips to the Hampshire Record Office, I have been unable to find many details of William Price himself. Infuriatingly, he appears to have left no diaries or accounts written in his own hand, and bequeathed his school no portraits or busts of himself, and none of his friends or business acquaintances recorded anything about the man. As I stated in the preface, the story below would never stand up in a court of law; it is conjecture, circumstantial evidence and hearsay. There is almost no corroboration between the components. Making many assumptions and with those caveats, I offer the following:

William's father, uncles and aunts grow up in Titchfield at about the same time as the shipwrights and timber merchants the Oxfords or Noxons live there, so perhaps William sen. is a friend or business acquaintance of theirs. By the time of William's sister Elizabeth's birth, the family have moved to Fareham. It's probably overly dramatic to suggest his father William. and his uncle John fight on opposite sides in the Civil War (Titchfield was Parliamentarian, Fareham Royalist), but it is possible.

In Fareham, his father works his trade as a master cooper from his shop and workhouse. The family is not rich, though well-off; they live in a comfortable home in Cams Oysell. He buys oak for the barrel staves from a local timber merchant - maybe the Oxfords, who can sell some that they would otherwise float downstream from Fareham quay to their shipyard in Weevil, Alverstoke. Perhaps William jun. plays with William Oxford, who was of the same age, while his father collected his timber. The strictures of puritanism stop them playing too boisterously, and no doubt both boys are expected to know and respect the teachings of the Church of England.

In 1660, there is elation in Fareham at the Restoration of the Monarchy and the return of Charles II to the throne. The following year, William sen. thinks it is a propitious time to become a man of property, and buys a couple of fields just off West Street.

In 1665, as William reached 14 and he would expect to apprentice himself to some master craftsman, the plague sweeps through Fareham, killing his father, and possibly leaving his sister weakened (about 20% of those infected survived). His widowed mother (or step-mother) Ann has to sell the land his father had invested in to pay their bequests - in particular the £10 William needs to buy his apprenticeship. As William knows the Oxfords, and they work with John Player who owns the Weevil brewery and cooperage in Alverstoke, perhaps he apprentices himself to them, leaving home to live with his master for the next seven years.

By 1673, William's apprenticeship is over, and he is back in Fareham, working for the Oxfords in the timber business. He is now legally able to marry, so in 1674 he and Mary Sewatt are wed in St Peter and St Paul's church. His trade takes him around the area evaluating, selecting and arranging to buy timber for the cooperage, the shipyard or for sale to the Royal Navy dockyard in Portsmouth. He probably travels on horseback, visiting the estates of Titchfield and Fareham and Southwick Parks.

In 1685, John Player dies and leaves his business to Henry Player. William decides to set out on his own, using his contacts to become a self-employed timber merchant supplying the Navy. He is now a member of the merchants' guild in Fareham, and beginning to move in influential circles, a considerable step up from his family background. He takes the wherry to the dockyard to negotiate contracts in between riding around to meet the land-owners' estate managers. The succession of wars meant the Navy's demand for new ships created a constant and very profitable stream of business, and William amasses a small fortune. Along with his merchant skills, he has accumulated financial acumen, and buys some lottery annuities for their high interest rates, as well as the new family home on West Street, near his father's old fields. Possibly he hears about Christ Church Hospital school through Samuel Pepys during business at the dockyard, and ponders the need for a charity school in Fareham.

Come 1695 and cousin John, in William's eyes the black sheep of the family because he was a Baptist, marries Deborah Walter in Portsmouth. They start a family, but their first son John dies in 1700. In 1706, Deborah's father Thomas dies. William is known to be wealthy and generous to his relatives, so John approaches him for a mortgage of £100 to start a cooperage business in his late father-in-law's old saddler's shop in Fareham.

Now aged 55, William is beginning to take things easier, having made his money, and reduces his timber trade with the Navy, and concentrates on his investments. By 1711 he starts buying rent-paying land with his savings, perhaps deciding to retire in a few years (anticipating by 230 years the 1946 National Insurance Act which established the retirement age of 65). Come 1719 he is not happy with the planned conversion of lottery annuities into South Sea Company shares, and finishes selling off his annuities by buying Daniell Waller's land in Elson. He has built a significant estate.

Now a part of the merchant and church establishment in Fareham, the borough court elects him bailiff from 1716 to 1720, though his comfortable old age is shattered by the death of Mary his wife in 1718. He writes his will at age 70 maybe reflecting a realisation that his biblical "three score years and ten" are up. His health is poor, (his will says "aged and weak in body", and a year earlier the court hearing his bill against Daniell Waller granted a *dedimus potestatem*) and he considers it time to establish his legacy. He is tired now, and finding the legal case with Waller a drain, he has to sell off the land he bought from Benjamin Bagster, but he does not remember to alter his will. He dies in 1725, a respected and admired businessman, if a hard man to cross.

Appendix A

Attorney General v. Price 1728

... Deborah Price and Wm. Price & John Woolgar combining and confederating to and with the Mr Barton Reeves Mr Wm. Green Mr John Gringoe & Mr Wm. Bennett and Diverse other persons to the Informant unknown ... to defeat the Charitable Devises refuse to execute any Conveyance of the reall Estate or assign such part of the personall Estate as is specifically devised to such Charitable uses ... – Attorney General v. Price

The Attorney General's words above appear to be a damning indictment. In actual fact, this seems to be standard phrasing of a purported wrong, and the Court of Chancery handled civil disputes over a range of subjects including land ownership and wills. It was not the court hearing cases of offences against the civil law, and hence it could not inflict punishment such as a prison sentence, only require legal remedies such as financial compensation or transfers of ownership to achieve equity.

Price's School always counted the 24th August 1721, the date on William Price jun.'s will, as its foundation date. However, the school certainly did not start before his death in 1725, and this legal bill "Attorney General v. Price" [TNA C 11/1012/2] brought before the Court of Chancery on 3rd February 1728 implies its inception did not run smoothly. At the time of this Bill, Price's house had been fitted out for a school, and the vicar and churchwardens had nominated a schoolmaster, and some pupils have been selected, but apparently not according the terms of the will.

The Bill seems to have arisen partly because opaque wording in Price's will and partly because circumstances changed between Price signing his will in 1721 and his death in 1725, but possibly greed also played a part. The plaintiffs were Daniel Wavell, vicar of Fareham, and Thomas Gover and William Rolfe, the churchwardens after Price's death. The defendants were Deborah, widow of John Price, their son William, and the churchwardens named in the will in 1721, John Woolgar, Barton Reeves, William Greene, John Gringoe and William Bennett. [For information, the author of this book believes he is not related to Thomas Gover despite sharing the same surname.]

A.1   The Bill and Answers

The Attorney General Sir Phillip York presented the Bill on behalf of Wavell, Rolfe and Gover. The two sides in the case agreed a number of points, listed below [To avoid confusion, "Price" in the following is William Price jun., and "William" is the son of John and Deborah Price.]

- the date, content and validity of the will, and Price's death on 21st May 1725, and John Woolgar as its legal executor;

- the will left the residue of Price's personal estate (that is to say money and property, as distinct from his real estate - land and buildings) to Woolgar, except for certain named items in the houses in West Street and Crockerhill;

- John Price, husband of Deborah, was the "John Price son of John Price" mentioned in the will, and was Price's legal heir; he had acknowledged the will as it required on 22nd June 1725, releasing him from the £100 mortgage and its interest;

- John died [he was buried on 17th August 1727] and John's will (see page 53) left his real estate to Deborah for her lifetime and thereafter to their son William;

- Price's will left the rents and income from land in Crockerhill and Elson to the charity school trustees - the vicar and churchwardens of Fareham and their successors;

- the will left the "persons named as Trustees for the erecting or forming a Charity School or their survivors" the £200 which remained owing from him on land in Crockerhill bought from Richard Lee [perhaps in 1708] to be paid when due, and 2 guineas each when the school was complete; and

- the will named the vicar of Fareham, Edward Jenkins (this was before his death in January 1722) and the churchwardens at the time, Barton Reeves, William Green, John Gringoe and William Bennett, and their survivors as trustees for fitting up the charity school.

The Attorney General expected the execution of the will to convey the land to the trustees, and the personal estate to be distributed according to will, but said that in fact:

- Deborah and William insisted John's will gave them title to the land Price intended for the charity school and refused to execute a conveyance of the land and personal estate to the charity;

- sometimes they claimed the will was improperly written, other times they claimed the "Minister and Churchwardens" were not a legal corporation and so they could not execute the conveyance without the court's intervention [the Attorney General conversely insists the conveyance is legal under the 1601 "Statute of Charitable Uses"];

- they claimed that Wavell, the vicar, lived at a distance from Fareham and employed a curate to officiate there, and that the curate should not be allowed as a trustee;

- they claimed that they needed the court's direction on how to select the school's pupils; and

- Woolgar claimed all the goods in Price's house and refused to transfer them as the will directed [again because the beneficiaries were not a corporation] and claimed the 2 guineas for each trustee was to be paid from the charity's income and not from Price's residual personal estate.

The defendants' Answers agree to follow the court's ruling on the points above, but claim in turn:

- the law required Wavell to live within the vicarage, and the will did not allow for the curate acting instead of the vicar as a trustee; Edward Jenkins lived in the vicarage and had no curate - the first instance of using a curate was Wavell - and so Price would not have considered whether a curate could act as trustee; and

- under Wavell, "no poor child is admitted to the school unless they can read the Bible in good measure", which excluded poor children whose parents could not afford to teach them.

In Answers to this Bill in May 1729 [TNA C 11/1019/2] the original named trustees, Bennett, Reeves, Gringo and Green claim:

- between writing his will and his death, Price sold the land he bought from Benjamin Bagster; and

- the defendants fitted up the school according to the will, but had received neither the £200 nor the 2 guineas each.

Finally in January 1730, John Woolgar submits a claim for expenses to the Court [TNA C 11/1020/2] asking whether the two guineas given each of the trustees could be paid out of the rents and profits bequeathed to the charity because Price's residual personal estate was insufficient after settling Price's debts owed at the time of his death.

A.2   Price's legacies

It is clear from this Bill that churchwardens named in 1721 thought they were to fit out Price's house as the school and receive £200 on its completion. They are not the only people to read the will this way - wooden "Charity Boards" describing Price's charity originally in St

Peter and St Paul's church, later in the entrance to Price's School, and most recently on the wall in Fareham College, say:

> *William Price, late of FAREHAM, Timber Merchant, by his will… bequeathed £200 to Trustees for the erecting and forming a Charity School in Fareham, and he gave his Land and Estate … Unto the Minister and Churchwardens of Fareham and their Successors for ever.*

However the Attorney General's interpretation as explained in the Bill is:

> *… he likewise willed that the sume of £200 which then remaind due from him on the Lands he purchased of Richard Lee in the tithing of Cockerhill in the parish of Fareham should immediately after his decease be put into the hands of the persons thereafter named for Trustees for the Executing or forming a Charity School in Fareham aforesaid should be thereinafter mentioned to be paid by them or the Survivours of them as soon as those two hundred pounds should become due*

As far as can be made out, this says that Price contracted to pay Lee a further £200 land purchase at some time in the future. Since Price left Lee's land to the charity, it would become liable for the debt, so he also left the trustees £200 to cover it, to be paid by them when it became due to Lee. If this is correct, and the court decided the same, it presumably came as a nasty shock to the trustees to discover their recompense for fitting out the school was 2 guineas each, and not £200 plus 2 guineas each!

There is another piece of either careful or casual wording in the will: he left his land for financing the school's operation to people specified by role:

> *unto the Minister and Churchwardens of the said parish of Fareham and their successors forever, the cleer Rents and profits of which shall be for the use of the said Charity Schoole,*

whereas he seems to have specified the trustees for setting up the school by name:

I doe hereby Constitute and make the Reverend Mr Edward Jenkins vicar of Fareham aforesaid Mr Barton Reeves Mr William Greene Mr John Gringoe, and Mr William Bennett all of Fareham afore- said and the Survivours and Survivour of them my Trustees for the fitting up of the said Charity School

Finally, we discover that Price had sold the land from Bagster which was part of the school's endowment and, at least according to Woolgar, Price's debts after his death left too little to pay the trustees their 2 guineas each. Maybe in the aftermath of Price's previous cases in Chancery he ran out of ready money. He brought the 1720 Bill against Daniel Waller over the purchase of the land in Elson (see page 74) where he may have been forced to pay interest on his late payment to Waller as well as hefty legal fees, and possibly had to defend an earlier Bill in 1716 - Twineham v. Price [TNA C 11/1348/20] - though this might be a totally different William Price.

We can wonder how much of the charity's money these cases wasted on legal fees. By the start of the 18th century, the Court of Chancery was notoriously expensive, and by the mid 19th century its corruption and inefficiency became the basis of Charles Dickens's "Bleak House". That said, the Court had one of several reforms in 1706, so perhaps it was not at its worst.

Appendix B

The Price wills

The following transcriptions break the text into several paragraphs, but the originals have no such breaks.

B.1 The will of William Price senior, cooper

We whose names are hereunto subscribed being present with William Price of Fareham in the County of South[ampt]on cooper on the eleaventh day of June Anno D[omi]ni 1665

The said William Price being sicke in body but of Sound and perfect memory Did declare & make his last will and testament said in these words following desiring us to put the same in writing; That is to say First and primirally I deliver my Soule into the hande of Almighty God my Creator and my body to the earthe from whence it was taken

Item I give and bequeath unto my Sonne William Price the some of Ten pounds for to bind him Apprentice

Item I give and bequeath unto my said Sonne William the table in my Hall & the Stooles to the said table belonging

Item I give and bequeath unto my daughter Elizabeth Price my best bedd and bedstead with all the furniture thereunto belonging now standing in the Chamber over the Hall, and whereas my said daughter Elizabeth is to receive out of the land which I have surrendered to my wife the Some of twenty pounds My will & desire is that if my said daughter shall happen to dye before shee shall attayne her full age of

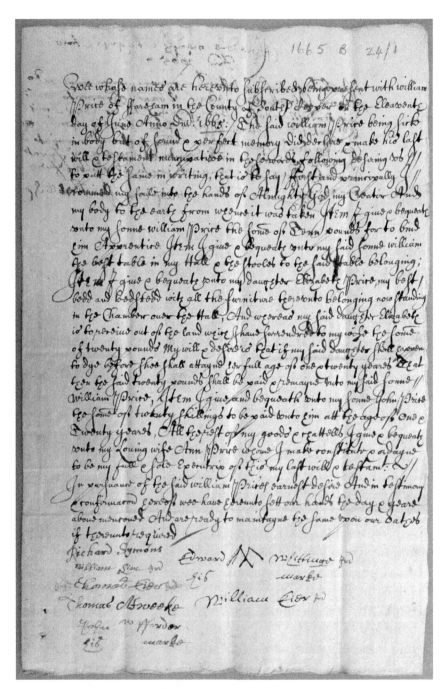

William Price senior's will; [HRO 1665B/24]

one & twenty yeares that then the said twenty pounds shall be paid & remayne unto my said Sonne William Price

Item I give and bequeath unto my Sonne John Price the Some of twenty shillings to be paid unto him at the age of one & twenty years

All the rest of my goodes & chattelles I give and bequeath unto my Loving wife Ann Price whome I make constitute & ordayne to be my full & Sole Executrix of this my last will & testament

& in persuance of the Said William Price's earnest desire And in testimony I confirm and hereof wee have hereunto sett our hands the day & yeare above mentioned and are ready to maintane the same upon our oathes if thereunto required

Richard Symons
Edward Whittinge *his marke*
William Lion
Thomas Eider
Thomas Atweeke
William Eier
John Forder *his marke*

B.2   Estate inventory of William Price senior

Fareham

An inventory of the Goods and Chattels of William Price
late of Fareham in the County of Southampton deceased,
taken the first day of July 1655
by Edward Whittinge the elder and Ralph Hoult
as follows:

All his wearing apparel, linen and woollens	£2-0-0
In the Chamber over the Hall	
An iron chest and a small table, a desk and coffer	£0-15-0
One basket chair and other chairs	£0-6-0
One carpet and a small basket	£0-3-4
In the Loft over the Kitchen	
An old saw, a small bed and a small chair and other linen box	£0-5-0
In the Hall	
A joint cupboard, a small iron table, two chairs, 4 cushions and a pair of augers	£1-0-0
Five pieces of pewter, two pewter candlesticks and two of brass, 3 salts, one pint pot and a candlepot of pewter, a lantern, an aconite bottle, 3 small earthenware dishes, 2 dozen trenchers and small glasses	£0-2-0
In the Chamber within the Hall	
One half-headed bedstead, mat and cord, one feather bed, a feather bolster and three pillows of feathers and a flock bed	£3-0-0
One coverlet, a pair of blankets and a pair of sheets	£0-16-0
A flock bed, a flock bolster, two flock pillows, a pare? blanket and coverlet	£0-15-6
Two warming pans, a feather pillow and a small chest	£0-13-0
4 pairs of sheets and one; 8 table glasses, 8 napkins, 6 pillow ties and other small linen	£1-13-4
In the Inner Buttery	
Fourteen pewter dishes, 4 porringers of pewter, two chamber pots, one salt and 3 saucers, 8 spoons	£1-0-0

In the Outer Buttery	
3 firkins, 2 half-firkins, 2 stanes?, 3 coffers, two forks, a frying pan and other lumber	£0-13-4
In the Kitchen	
One table and frame, a small table and form, 4 chairs	£0-13-0
One brass pot, 2 kettles, two skillets, a skewer and ladle of brass, one mortar	£1-0-0
Two firing? pots, a fire pan and tongs, one cotterell?, a pair of small dogs, one spit, two pair of pothooks	£0-11-0
A furnace and a pair of bellows	£0-10-0
One tobe [tub?], a bucket, a half bushel, a brush, a range? with other lumber	£0-5-6
In the Shop	
All his working tools, 5 dozen of hoops and a parcel of small timber	£1-10-0
In the Loft over the Shop	
4 dozen of hoops, a small parcel of timber	£0-6-0
In the Work House and Backside	
Two hundredweight and some odd boards of hogshead	£1-0-0
3 hundredweight and a half of shingles	£1-4-0
A parcel of old timber newly bought at Portsmouth	£1-5-0
A parcel of broken timber and 7 dozen and a half of hoops	£0-7-8
A small grinding stone	£0-4-0
Timber in the Street	£1-2-0
Field 3 acres of barley	£3-0-0
Sum total	**£27-2-8**

Edward Whittinge *his mark*
Ralph Holt

Notes

The preceding table is translated into modern terminology, apart from words marked with a "?" for which I have been unable to discover a meaning or am otherwise unsure of.

This inventory makes very difficult reading - see the extract on this page. It is written in "secretary hand" and suffers not only from the usual lack of standard spelling in the 17th century, but also from the main author, Edward Whittinge, being semi-literate - he makes his mark on the inventory, rather than signing it. It contains many spelling mistakes and inconsistencies, and of course uses terms no longer in use.

Part of the inventory; [HRO 1665B 24/2]

in the woorke house and backside

Itm. to cwt and som od boardes of hogesheed-i£-0-0

3 cwt. and a hafe of shengells—i-4-0

a pasell of owlld timber newly
bought at porchmauth—}-i-5-0

Itm. a passel of broken timber and
7 dussen and a haffe of hoopes-}0-7-8

The following list of terms may be of use:

Coffer a wooden storage box, usually standing on the floor.

Joint cupboard is joinery, i.e all wooden.

Auger a wood drill that seems to have escaped from the workshop.

A salt is a box containing the condiment.

Aconite from the Monkshood alias Wolfsbane plant was used as a medicine. These days it is considered a very powerful and dangerous poison.

Trencher a wooden plate used for everyday meals.

Bedstead listed in the inventory as a "bedsteadall", a contraction of "bed steadall", a bed frame - nowadays further contracted to "bedstead".

Cords across bed frames suspended the mattress; other forms of beds used planks for support.

Flock i.e. wool or cloth scraps, a cheaper and coarser filling than feathers. Richer people had feather mattresses over flock or straw filled ones.

Porringer a bowl suitable for porridge or soup.

Buttery the room where you kept your butts - that is, bottles of drink and barrels of beer, the latter taking the place of today's tea or coffee as refreshment.

Chamber pots used in the days before the outside privy and mains drainage, and kept in the house as a convenience.

Firkin a 9-gallon storage barrel, not just a measure of beer, and we can be sure a cooper's house would have a ready supply of them for foodstuffs such as flour. Alternatively, this could just be some stock escaped from the shop.

A range in the kitchen implies they were well-off trendsetters; ranges only became common a century or so later.

Backside presumably the part of William's land behind the house, shop and workhouse.

Hoops William's stock included 16 dozen hoops, enough for about 32 barrels, as each requires 6 hoops.

The inventory is consistent with William sen. being a well-off artisan living in a comfortably-furnished small two-roomed (kitchen plus hall) cottage with an upper storey. Normally the "chamber over the hall" would be a bedroom, rather than what seems to be an office. Having beds within the hall was not unusual in earlier times; perhaps William was a traditionalist.

Edward Whittinge was one of the witnesses to William's will; it is a surprise to find him performing the inventory, which is the responsibility of the executor. The will named William's wife Ann as executor.

B.3 The will of William Price junior, timber merchant

In the name of God Amen the Twenty Fourth day of August in the yeare of our Lord One Thousand Seaven hundred and Twenty one, And in the Eighth yeare of his Ma[jes]ties reigne etc. I William Price of the parish of Fareham in the County of South[amp]ton Timber Merchant being aged and weak in Body, but of Sound and perfect mind memory and understanding Doe make publish and declare this my Last will and Testament in manner and forme following that is to say

First I Comend my Soule to God and my Body to the Earth to be buried in a Decent manner under the Stone my Father and mother Lye in Fareham Church yard

Item All those my messuages or tenements with Thappurtanc[e]s scituate and being in the parish of Portsea in the Said County which I purchased of William Bragg I give and bequeath unto Mary Enon the wife of Thomas Enon for and during the Terme of her naturall life And after her decease I give and bequeath the said Messuages or Tenements and p[re]myses to Thomas Enon their Son and his heires for ever.

Item I give unto my Executor hereafter named all my Household goods in my now dwelling house in Fareham aforesaid Except those hereafter ment[i]oned which shall be left as Standards to the said House viz. One Furnace One Leaden pump One Clock and Case one Large Table in the parlour the Hangings in Both Chambers the Fire Hearth and all the Standes Dressers and Shelves belonging to the said House.

Item All those my Coppyhold Lands with Thappurtanc[e]s called Butterwick with the Small Purrock thereto adjoining which I purchased of Mrs Mooring Lyeing within the Mannor of Fareham (which said Coppyhold Lands as well as the other Lands hereinafter ment[i]oned scituate and being within the said Mannor I have surrendred to the use of my Last will and Testament) I give and bequeath unto my kinsman Thomas Price the son of Peter Price and his heires forever according to the Custom of the said Mannor, he and they paying thereout the severall Legacys following viz

To his sister Mary Bryant the wife of Thomas Bryant the sume of

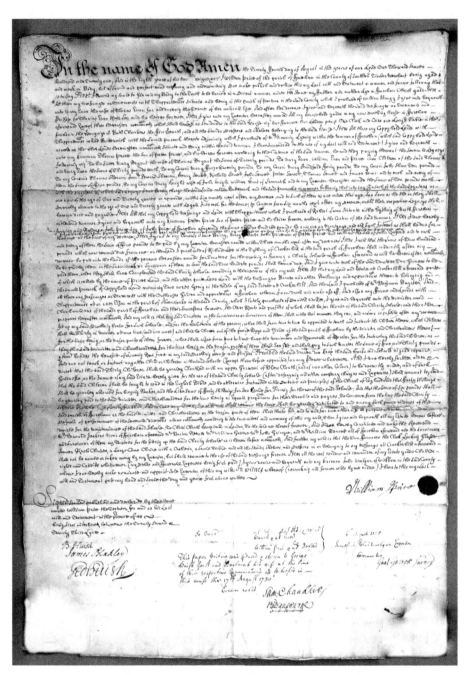

William Price junior's will; [HRO 1725B/52]

Twenty pounds, To Mary Enon, William Enon and Price Enon Children
of the said Thomas and Mary Enon the sume of Thirty pounds each, To
my cousin Mary Furze Twenty pounds, To my cousin Mary Bradford
Forty pounds To my cousin John Shaw Ten pounds To my Cousins
Thomas Sherwin jun & Edward Sherwin, Henry Sewett, Richard Sewett,
John Sewett, Peter Sewett, Thomas Sewett and James Hunt and to each
and every of them the sum of Five pounds. To my cousins Mary Knight
wife of John Knight William Hunt of Swannick and to my Executor
hereafter named the sume of Ten pounds each

with the payment of which said Legacys I doe hereby charge the
said Lands called Butterwick and the said purroke in manner following
that is to say, To such of the said Legatees as are now of the age of One
and Twenty yeares or upwards, within six months next after my decease
and to such of them as are under that age soe soon as he she or they
shall severally attaine to the age of One and Twenty yeares with Legall
Interest for the same to comence from six months next after my decease
until their respective Legacys shall become due and payable

Item All that my Coppyhold Messuage and Lands with Thappur-
tance's which I purchased of Robert Swan scituate within the Tything
of North Fareham with[i]n said Mannor I give and bequeath unto my
kinsman Peter Price son of Peter Price and his heires forever according
to the Custom of the said Mannor

Item I doe hereby forgive and Release John Price Son of John Price
of Fareham afforsaid the sume of One hundred pounds he ows me on
Mortgage and all such Interest as shall be due for {*provided the said John
Price doe within Three months next after my decease acknowled[g]e this my will
by some writing under his hand & Seale to be duely made and Executed for that
purpose*} the same at the time of my decease.

Item I give to my Cousins Anne Barry, Mary Palmer John Price son
of Peter Price and William the son of John Oxford and to such and every
of them the Sume of Five pounds to be paid by my Executor hereafter
named within Three months next after my decease.

Item I will the Sume of Two hundred pounds which now remains
due from me on the Land I purchased of Richard Lee of the Tything
of Crocker hill in the said parish of Fareham shall imediatly after my decease be putt into the hands of the persons hereafter named for Trustees

for the erecting or Forming a Charity Schoole in Fareham aforsaid as will be hereinafter men[t]ioned to be paid by them or the Survivors or Survivour of them as soon as the said Two hundred pounds shall become due, And I give unto each of the said Executors Two Guineas to be paid them when they shall have Compleated the said Charity Schoole according to the direc[t]ions of this my will

Item All that my Land and Estate att Crocker hill aforsaid parte of which is called by the name of Prices Land, and the other parte Lees Land with the Messuages Barnes and other Buildings and appurten[a]nces thereunto belonging and the small purrock of Coppyhold Land containing Two acres lyeing in the midle of my said Estate att Crocker hill, And the Land I purchased of Mr Benjamin Bagster, And all those my Messuages or Tenements with the Outhouses Garden and appurten[en]cs in Fareham where in I now dwell and make use of, And alsoe my Farme and Lands with Thappurtences at or near Elson in the parish of Alverstoake in the said County, which I lately purchased of Daniell Waller, I give and bequeath unto the Minister and Churchwardens of the said parish of Fareham and their successors forever, the cleer Rents and profits of which shall be for the use of the said Charity Schoole, and the other purposes hereafter mentioned,

And my will is that my said Trustees or the Suvivours or Survivour of them, shall in the best manner they can, and as soon as possible after my decease fitt up my said Dwelling house for such Schoole, and for the habitat[i]on of the person who shall from time to time be appointed to teach and Instruct the Children therein, which Children shall be Thirty in number att one time (and noe more) and shall be chosen ou[t] of the poore Boys and Girles of the said parish of Fareham by the Minister and Churchwardens thereof for the time being, or the major parte of them forever, who shall alsoe from time to time have the Nominac[i]on and Removeall of a Master for the Instructing the said Children, as they the said Minister and Churchwardens for the time being or the Ma[j]or parte of them shall See fitt, and shall pay to such Master the sume of Five and Thirty pounds p[er] A[nnu]m besides the benefit of Living Rent free in my said Dwelling Hous and p[re]misses Provided the said Master doe keep the said Hous and Schoole in good repaire, And doe not teach or Instruct any other Child or Children in the said Schoole

(Except those before appointed) on any p[re]tence whatsoever

And I doe hereby further order & direct that the said Thirty Children shall be yearley Cloathed with an upper Garment of Blew Cloath (and of noe other Colour) to be decently made and of such Goodness as the Income of my said Estate hereby given for the use of the said Charity Schoole (after defraying all other necessary charges and Expences) shall amount to, And that the said Children shall be taught to read in the English Bible, and be otherwise Instructed in the Doctrine and Principles of the Church of England And that Forty shillings shall be yearely allowed for buying Bookes, and the Like sume of Forty shillings for Sea Coale for Fireing for the use of the said Schoole, And that the sume of Six pounds shall be yearely paid to the said Minister and Churchwardens for the time being in Equall propor[t]ion for their Trouble and paynes, To Comence from the time the said Charity Schoole shall be Compleatly finished, And in Case any Overplus of Rents shall remaine the same shall be yearely distributed to and among such poore widows of the said parish of Fareham as the said Minister and Churchwardens or the major parte of them shall thinke fit, and to and for noe other use or purpose whatsoever.

And in Default of performance of the severall direcc[i]ons above men[t]ioned according to the true intent and meaning of this my will, Then I give and bequeath all my Estate herein before devised for the maintainance of the said Schoole To Christ Church Hospital in London, To the Sole use thereof forever, And I doe hereby Constitute and make the Reverend Mr Edward Jenkins vicar of Fareham aforsaid Mr Barton Reeves Mr William Greene Mr John Gringoe, and Mr William Bennett all of Fareham aforsaid and the Survivours and Survivour of them my Trustees for the fitting up of the said Charity School as is hereinbefore men[t]ioned, And further my will is that the Two Furnaces the Clock, Looking Glasses Seaven Rush Chaires, a Large Cane Chaire with a Cusheron, a Small Table and all the Stands, Shelves and Dressers in or belonging to my messuages att Crockerhill aforsaid shall not be moved or taken away by my Exector, but shall remaine to the use of the said messuage forever

Item all the rest residue and remainder of my Estate goods Chattles rights and Creditts whatsoever (my Debts and Funerall Expences being first paid) I give devise and bequeath unto my kinsman John Woolgar of Wickham in the said County whome I doe hereby make noninate and appoint Sole Executor of this my will

In witnes whereof (revoaking all former wills by me made) I have to this my Last will and Testament putt my hand and Seale the day and yeare first above written William Price

Signed sealed published and declared by the above named William Price the Testator for and as his Last will and Testament in the p[re]sence of us *being first interlined betweene the Twenty Second & Twenty Third Lynes*

B Huish
James Blakley
Geo[rge] Huish

B.4   Price's endowment

> *the erecting or Forming a Charity Schoole in Fareham ... the said Thirty Children shall be yearley Cloathed with an upper Garment of Blew Cloath (and of noe other Colour) to be decently made and of such Goodness as the Income of my said Estate hereby given for the use of the said Charity Schoole (after defraying all other necessary charges and Expences) shall amount to*

William Price's will endowed his charity with four pieces of land, though he had sold one by the time he died. He left other significant legacies of land - Butterwick and land in North Fareham to his kinsmen, and land in Portsea to the Enons.

The largest bequest to the charity was the land in Elson; the "Charity Boards" list it as just over 100 acres - this roughly agrees with the 1840 Tithe Apportionment, but that was after the Trustees of Price's Charity sold Priddy's Hard, another 44 acres, to the Board of Ordnance. Next largest was the land in Crockerhill, forming part of what is now called Charity Farm. Price also bought land from Benjamin Bagster, and left it to the charity, but we know from the Bill in Chancery that it was sold before his death. The last part of Price's endowment to the charity was

Location	Acres	Beneficiary
Portsea	?	Mary, wife of Thomas Enon, then their son Thomas
Butterwick	19	Thomas son of Peter Price
North Fareham	7½	Peter Price son of Peter Price
Crockerhill	52	Price's Charity
Bagster's land	?	Price's Charity, but sold before Price's death
Home in Fareham		Price's Charity
Elson	153	Price's Charity

his home on West Street. In terms of size this was negligible, just under ¼ acre.

Price's Charity endowment was thus about 205 acres of land.

B.5 Bluecoat schools

The will's specification of an *"upper Garment of Blew cloth"* to be provided makes it clear William knew all about the movement creating bluecoat schools and that his school should be one of them.

Books on the subject say there was no single project to set up bluecoat schools - rather, a consensus in the merchant class to do charitable works. The Society for the Promotion of Christian Knowledge (the SPCK), founded in 1698, was an integral part and possible catalyst of this. Many of these books say that the use of blue cloth was because it was cheap and marked the poor children out, and the motivation behind the schools was to provide the middle-class merchants with stream of docile working-class labour. Such arguments seem almost vindictive in their rejection of any charitable aspect to the movement, and tied to a far-left political dogma. It is clear from the will that William Price was specifying good clothing and shoes for the school's pupils; the blue was not to mark out the poor as cheaply as possible. It was to be the best the charity could afford, and if he wanted merely to ensure a stream of labourers, would he not have specified some more vocational teaching, or even left his money to found a police force?

William's specification for the schoolmaster is not as tightly drawn as that specified by the SPCK. According to the *Encyclopaedia of Education*, they wanted:

> *a member of the Church of England, of a sober life and conversation, and not under the age of 25 years; one that frequents the Holy Communion; one that hath a good government of himself and passions; one of a meek temper and humble behaviour; one of a good genius for teaching; one who understands well the grounds and principles of the Christian religion; ... one who can write a good hand, and who understands the grounds of arithmetic; one who keeps good orders in his family*

whereas William just left the employment of the master to the charity trustees. While the SPCK's rules did cover the provision of coats and shoes, it did not suggest any particular colours.

Some movement to establish charity schools clearly had an effect: many bluecoat schools were founded in the period 1700-1725 (the *Encyclopaedia of Education* lists an increase in the number of charity schools from 254 in 1709 to 1,097 by 1720), and their uniforms almost always aped that of the Christ's Hospital School. There must have been some organizing force that caused them all to specify a similar uniform, but it has yet to be identified. William Price was aware of Christ's Hospital School; surely he and the other merchants establishing these schools were inspired by a lecture or pamphlet by someone from the school.

Appendix C

Forestry and timber

William Price's work as a timber merchant would be to contract to provide loads of wood in various categories. The Navy's warships required several distinct types of timber:

Knees the L- or V-shaped strengthening pieces for corner joints such as between hull and deck;

Oak planks for forming the hull and as armour (a 6" thick plank of seasoned oak can withstand a canon-ball), 50 feet in length; while the acute angle of knees required wood with the appropriate bend, a Royal Society paper of 1722 records immersing planks in heated sand to soften them for bending to fit ships' hulls;

A stand of oaks fit for planks

Softwood planks for interior decking, walls and interior hull, perhaps 40 feet in length;

Scantling odd smaller pieces for all the other things that ships need; and

Masts tall and perfectly straight wood, almost always imported.

An oak suitable for knees

Unmanaged trees in open spaces produce the multiple side branches with many bends that are so characteristic of the typical English oak beloved by garden designers like Capability Brown.

The various sorts of timber require different times before becoming ready for felling - softwoods in about 40 years, but oak needs at least 100 years. This has hampered scientific analysis of forestry over the years - few researchers are keen to embark on experiments that will not complete within their lifetime.

It seems that in Price's time, even less was known about arboriculture, or if it was known, it was rarely acted upon. The book plate used to illustrate the section on the timber trade on page 32 comes from *The Modern Druid* by James Wheeler (1747). That dealt exclusively with pruning and cutting operations to persuade an oak to grow without side branches in some desired form (straight or bent), at the cost of considerable repeated labour. It contained no indication of planting to produce the appropriate growth.

Rather than use forest management to produce the required types and amount of timber, the strategy was simply to search the forests to find appropriate trees. Henry VIII passed an Act giving the Navy ownership of all suitable oak; the Navy's surveyor would travel the forest putting the "King's mark" on suitable trees, which could no longer be felled except by the Navy's order. This strategy only works, of course, when supply exceeds demand, as the land cleared by felling a tree will be repopulated at random by unsuitable trees.

The Navy was aware of this lack of knowledge, and commissioned an investigation which resulted in the first report by the new Royal Society. The resulting book, *Sylva, or, A discourse of forest-trees, and the propagation of timber in His Majesties dominions* by John Evelyn, well-known for his diaries, was published in 1662. Its main planting recommendations are more to do with soils, location and means of transplanting than any considerations of yield or size. Its recommendation for timber trees is to plant at least 40 foot apart, which we now know encourages spread at the expense of height.

Modern forest management for timber production plants "stands" of oak, pine etc. and manage them to produce the desired style and quality of timber. For the most used category, planks, the goal is a tall, straight trunk with no side branches. This is achieved by planting seedlings close together, and then thinning out as they gain height. This causes the young plants to compete to get the light, so they grow upwards fast, with a comparatively small crown at the top. Different species get planted between the oaks to manage this competition and to exclude light from the trunks to discourage side branches - and any that do grow are pruned off. Trees for masts and poles are managed in the same way, but with faster-growing species, giving intense competition leading to straight trunks.

Closely planted softwood growing tall and straight

Appendix D

The Price's School badge

The school badge is in heraldic terms "sable, a lion rampant regardant, argent; a staff wreathed fesswise in the same", a silver lion facing backwards over his shoulder and standing on two feet over a staff on a black background. (The nearest heraldic "tincture" is sable; azure is a rather paler blue than the school badge.) The "lion rampant regardant" appears in the Ceridigon (formerly Cardiganshire) flag, in gold on black; it appears in several Welsh coats of arms.

Price's School badge

A Reverend William Price born in 1663 and educated in Oxford, had a son Roger who moved to America to be the incumbent of King's Chapel, Boston, Massachusetts. *The Annals of King's Chapel*, Henry Wilder Foote (1882) shows his coat of arms on Page 388, "sable, lion rampant regardant; or" (a gold lion on a black background). Not only does this shield show our lion, but the demi lion above it has stands on the same ragged staff as the school badge. Maybe a Victorian trustee chose it for the school badge, but it is like an overly-expensive bottle of wine: the right vintage but the wrong Price.

Roger Price's coat of arms

William Price's seal

William Price signed and sealed his will in 1721, and his seal shows a lion. It is a "Lion Passant Guardant" in heraldic terms, facing towards us and with all paws except the front right on the ground, surmounted by a crest of a plume of feathers. This is nothing like the school's badge. Lovers of pub quiz trivia will be pleased to know that a lion passant guardant is also known as a "Leopard" in heraldry. According to *The Oxford Guide to Heraldry* (1988), quoting Bado Aureo, a leopard was *"borne of an adulterous union between a lioness and a pard and like a mule incapable of reproducing, a leopard may be an appropriate charge for a person born of adultery or barred from reproducing (such as an abbot)"*. Of course, this "leo-pard" is from the mediaeval bestiary, not modern zoology, and neither it nor the "pard" are any more real than dog-headed men or unicorns.

Appendix E

List of Prices in 17th Century Hampshire

This list contains all members of Price families baptised before 1700 according to findmypast.com and the Titchfield History Society's transcription of the parish records in 2020. It contains a few other people for completeness. It lists parents first, then children with their baptism dates. Marriage dates and wives' surnames are given when known. As the name "Price" is an Anglicisation of the Welsh patronymic "ap Rhys", it is a common surname for people with Welsh ancestry. Therefore, the Prices listed are unlikely to be William Price's relatives without corroborating evidence. In summary:

- 197 people surnamed Price, including 32 Johns, 21 Williams, 17 Marys, 10 Elizabeths, 10 Roberts, 9 Thomases, 7 Peters and only 1 Charles;

- 36 distinct Price families, fathers: 15 John Prices, 9 William Prices and 4 Thomas Prices;

- the largest family is Ellis Price and Ann Rathborne's in Gatcombe, Isle of Wight, with 14 children baptised between 1624 and 1642;

- 61 Prices baptised in 10 families in Titchfield; and

- 35 people baptised in 10 families on the Isle of Wight.

E.1 Fareham, Titchfield and Bishop's Waltham

Fareham St Peter & St Pauls'

- Petter Price; Peeter Price 1643.

- Peeter & Elizabeth Price; Peter 1661, Elizabeth 1663-1663, John 1665, Robart 1674, Mary 1676, Elizabeth 1678.

- William (William Price sen.) 1617-1665 & Ann Price; Elizabeth 1649. William (William Price jun.) 1651-1725, John 1662.

- John Price & unknown; Mary 1667.

- William Price (William Price jun.) 1651-1725 & Mary Sewatt 1649-1718 m: 1674.

Titchfield St Peter's

- John Prise & Margaret Waller m: 1601; John 1602, Nicholas 1605-1608, Christopher 1609-1684 (see Bishop's Waltham), Marcy 1611, William (William Price sen.) 1617-1665; Sarah 1619; Frances 1622-1622, Ellen 1624.

- Nicholas Price ?-1610 & unknown; Marcye 1606, John 1608.

- John Price jun. 1602 (above) & unknown; John 1632, Peeter 1633, Will 1636. Will may be the husband William of Sarah Bassat below.

- Robert Prise & Barbery Hills m: 1633; Jane 1636, Agnis 1638, Robert 1640, William 1644. William may be the husband of Agnes Winter below.

- John Price (John Price sen.) 1632-1719 & Ann Cortnell m: 1670; John 1671-1673, Marey 1672, Mary 1673, John 1674.

- Peter Price & Ann Knight m: 1642; Peeter 1643. Peter may be William Price sen.'s brother.

- John Price (possibly John Price jun. above or the collier below) & unknown; Dorathey 1643.

- John Price the collier & unknown: Alice 1641, Sibbell 1647.

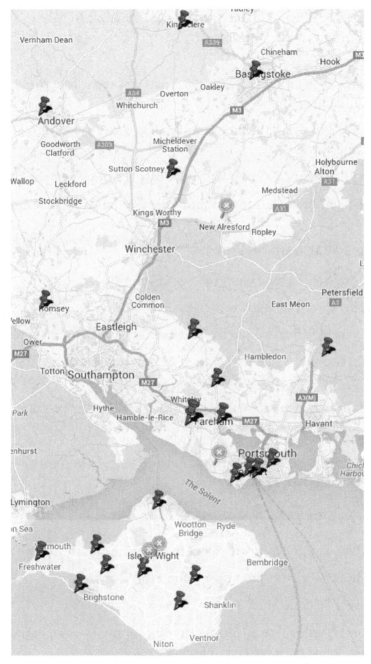

Map of Hampshire parishes with Prices resident
Map © OpenStreetMap contributors

- Peter & Elizabeth Price - the same Peter and Elizabeth as in Fareham above. Peter may be Peeter born 1643 to Peter Price & Ann Knight.
- Peter & Joan Price: Peter 1661, Joan 1665-1665, Ralph 1667, William 1677.
- Peter Price of Sarisbury or Swannick; Mary 1669, John 1672, Robert 1676.
- William Price & Sarah Bassat m: 1665; a son 1669-1669.
- William Price & Agnes Winter m: 1670; Jane 1671, Sarah 1674.

Bishop's Waltham St Peter's

- John Price & Jane Cutler m: 1629; John 1630.
- John Sewatt & unknown; Alice 1631, Mary 1634.
- Richard Sewet & Martha Leach m: 1633; Richard 1634, John 1649.
- Christopher Price 1609-1684 & Mary Greetom m: 1636; Nicholas 1637, Mary 1640, Sarah 1644.
- Henry Sewatt & Ursula Allen m: 1638; Ursula 1641-1641, Elizabeth 1648. Mary 1649-1718, Richard 1650.

E.2   Further afield

Alverstoke St Mary's

- Thomas Price & Joane Hicks m: 1607; Elizabeth 1606, Joane 1609.
- Thomas Price & unknown; John 1636, Robert 1637.
- Israel Price & Mary Printon m: 1679; Mary 1679.
- John & Sarah Price; Elizabeth 1687, John 1688-1689, Sarah 1690, William 1692, John 1695, Thomas 1699.
- Robert & Joan Price; Robert 1678-1678, Robert 1683, Thomas 1685.

- Simon & Mary Price; Mary 1690.

- John & Mary Price; Mary 1696.

Andover

- David Price & unknown; Mary 1612.

Basingstoke

- Elizabeth Price 1640.

Charlton

- William Price 1579; took oath of allegiance before sailing to Low Countries 1618.

Gosport Holy Trinity

- John Price & Jane Kirby m: 1697 in Portsmouth; Catherine 1698, John 1700.

Kingsclere St Mary's

- Matthias Price & unknown; Jane 1646.

Micheldever St Mary the Virgin

- James & Elizabeth Price; Agnes 1541.

Old Alresford St Mary the Virgin

- William Price & Luce Scriven m: 1592.

Portsea St Mary's

- Thomas Enon & Mary Bradford 1689-1728 m: 1712 Rowner; Thomas 1712, William 1714-1714, Mary 1715, William 1718, Price 1721.

Portsmouth St Thomas of Canterbury

- Cornelius Price 1624 & Elizabeth Knight m: 1671; Anne 1674.

- John Price & Mary Martin m: 1680; John 1688, Christian 1692.

- John Price (John Price jun.) 1674-1727 & Deborah Walter m: 1695; Deborah, William ~1702.

- Thomas Price & Mary Blundell m: 1683; Mary 1681.

- William & Elizabeth Price; Elizabeth 1694, Sarah 1699, Mary 1700.

- John & Elizabeth Price; John 1698.

- Thomas & Jane Price; Jane 1700.

Rockbourne St Andrew's

- Evan Price & Amie Keylweye (Kenwyn?) m 1581; Thomas 1581, Margaret 1584, Ellis 1588, Alice 1589. William 1592, Andrew 1595.

Romsey

- Raphe Price & unknown; Anne 1627.

E.3 Isle of Wight

Brook St Mary the Virgin

- Joanne Price 1604.

Calbourne All Saints'

- Arthur Price (possibly m: 1606 Jane Wyn); William 1619, Frances 1621. Edward 1622, Jane 1623. Elizabeth 1625, Mary 1627.

Cowes St Mary the Virgin

- John Price & unknown; Mary 1688-1689, Mary 1690.

Gatcombe St Olave's

- Ellis Price & Ann Rathborne m: 1624; John 1624, Theodore 1625, Sampson 1627, William 1628, Abraham 1629, Katherine 1630, Ann 1631, Dorothy 1632, Ellis 1633, Peter 1635-1635, Morgan 1636, Thomas 1639, Henry 1641, Richard 1642.

Godshill All Saints'

- Charles Price; Mary 1698.

Newchurch All Saints'

- Richard Price & unknown; Richard 1700.

Newport Minster Church of St Thomas

- John Price & Jeane Boyes m: 1632.

Shalfleet St Michael's

- Robert Price & unknown; Joan 1621, Elizabeth 1624.

Yarmouth St James'

- John Price & Mary Luttery m: 1641 in Carisbrook; John 1642, Jane 1645.
- John & Jane Price; Mary 1647, Robert 1650.
- Richard & Jane Price; William 1667.
- Robert & Jeane Price; Jeane 1691, Mary 1694.

Index of family members, surnames, etc.

Printed in Great Britain
by Amazon

42737693R00077